Ecosystem Services
Come to Town

Ecosystem Services Come to Town

Greening cities by working with nature

Gary Grant

A John Wiley & Sons, Ltd., Publication

Registered Office
John Wiley & Sons, Ltd, The Atrium, Southern Gate, Chichester, West Sussex, PO19 8SQ, UK

Editorial Offices
9600 Garsington Road, Oxford, OX4 2DQ, UK
The Atrium, Southern Gate, Chichester, West Sussex, PO19 8SQ, UK
2121 State Avenue, Ames, Iowa 50014-8300, USA

For details of our global editorial offices, for customer services and for information about how to apply for permission to reuse the copyright material in this book please see our website at www.wiley.com/wiley-blackwell.

Library of Congress Cataloging-in-Publication Data

Grant, Gary, 1958–
    Ecosystem services come to town : greening cities by working with nature / by Gary Grant.
        pages   cm
    Includes bibliographical references and index.
    ISBN 978-1-4051-9506-5 (pbk. : alk. paper)
1. City planning–Environmental aspects.   2. Sustainable urban development.   I. Title.
    NA9053.E58G73 2012
    711'.4–dc23
                                                            2012006681

A catalogue record for this book is available from the British Library.

Wiley also publishes its books in a variety of electronic formats. Some content that appears in print may not be available in electronic books.

Set in 10/12.5pt Avenir by SPi Publisher Services, Pondicherry, India
Printed and bound in Malaysia by Vivar Printing Sdn Bhd

Cover design by Andy Meaden
Cover image shows Phoenix Garden in London's West End. Photograph by Gary Grant

1   2012

Contents

About the Author   xi

Acknowledgement   xiii

1. Introduction   1
   Modern Cities and the Disconnected   1
   Population Spike   2
   Limits to Growth   3
   Global Threats   3
   Ecosystem Services and Stewardship   4
   Greening Cities is Necessary   5
   Hope   5

2. Origins of Cities   7
   Why Look Back?   7
   Emergence of the Human Species   7
   Great Leap Forward   8
   Agriculture and Permanent Settlements   8
   Agriculture Around the World   10
   Agriculture Intensifies   11
   Empires Rise and Fall in Mesopotamia   12
   Nile Valley   12
   Indus Valley   13
   Ancient China   13
   Ancient Greece   14
   On the Ganges   15
   Rome   16
   The Moche   16
   Mesoamerica   17
   Fortified Centres of Administration   17
   European Renaissance   18
   Early Modern   19
   Squalor   21

3. Modern Cities   23
   Origins of the Modern City   23
   Industrial Revolution   23
   Railways   24
   Rapid Growth   25

	Ill Health	26
	Distinctive New Districts Emerge	27
	Paris Re-born	28
	Railways and Suburbs	29
	Planning and Zoning	29
	Garden Cities	29
	Motor Vehicles Herald in the Oil Age	31
	A Humane Outlook	32
	Going Up	33
	Continued Rise of the Motor Vehicle	33
	Decline of the Inner City	34
	New Towns	35
	City Plans	36
	An Unfinished Task	37
4.	**Issues Facing Contemporary Cities**	39
	Impacts of Cities and City Living	39
	Habitat Loss	40
	Habitat Fragmentation	41
	Impacts on Soil	41
	The Water Cycle	42
	Water-borne Pollution	44
	Urban Heat Islands	44
	Air Pollution	45
	Noise	46
	Light Pollution	47
	Agricultural Land Take	47
	Concrete	48
	Steel	48
	Glass	49
	Timber	49
	Waste	49
	Drivers of Population Growth	50
	Peak Oil	52
	Peak Phosphorus	52
	Post Oil	53
5.	**Working with Nature**	55
	Ecology and Ecosystems	55
	Born Free	56
	Saving the Great Lakes	56
	Earth Summit, Ecosystem Assessment and Ecosystem Services	58
	Cities as Part of the Biosphere	59
	Ecological Restoration	59
	Urban Wildlife	60
	Green Infrastructure	60

Sustainable Sites Initiative   61
Advice from Professional Bodies and Others   61
Mimic Nature   62
Working with Nature Works   63

6. Urban Nature   65
    Open Space Preservation   65
    The Naturalists   66
    Nature Leaves the City?   66
    Urban Nature Returns   68
    Wildlife Gardens   69
    Encapsulated Countryside   70
    Bukit Timah   71
    The Urban Forest   72
    Urban Wastelands   73
    Canvey Wick   74
    Emscher Park   75
    Urban Farming   76
    Biodiversity Action Plans   77
    River Corridors   78
    London's South Bank   79
    Minneapolis Riverfront   79

7. Water and Cities   81
    Fresh Clean Water – Essential and Increasingly Scarce   81
    Civilisation has Modified the Water Cycle   82
    Water Consumption   82
    Embodied Carbon   82
    Virtual Water   83
    Catchment Management   84
    Rainwater Harvesting   84
    Grey Water   85
    Sustainable Urban Drainage   85
    Water Sensitive Urban Design   86
    Rain Gardens   86
    The Streets are Changing   86
    Ponds   88
    Potsdamer Platz   89
    River Restoration   89
    The Cheonggyecheon River   90
    Singapore   91
    Water and Urban Heat Islands   93
    Towards the Water Sensitive City   93

8. City-wide Greening   95
    Bioregions   95
    Catchment Management for Clean Water   96

Catchment Management for Ecosystem Services 97
Regional Green Infrastructure Plans 99
Biomass and the Bioregion 99
Regional Ecological Networks 100
Community Forests 101
Green Belts 101
Green Grids 103
Transport 103
Urban Heat Islands 105
Blue Networks 105
Masterplanning 107
Regional Plans, Local Implementation 107

9. Greening Neighbourhoods and Buildings 111
Sense of Neighbourhood 111
Living Streets 112
Standardising the Neighbourhood 113
Design Your Own Park 113
A Phoenix Rises 114
Growing Their Own 115
Learning from Squatter Settlements 116
Rain Gardens 117
They Paved Paradise 118
Clapton Park Estate 118
People of the Trees 119
Tree Pits 120
Tree Trenches 121
No Space? 122
Energy Efficient Buildings 123
Water Efficiency 123
Autonomy 123
Building-integrated Vegetation 124
A Coat for Buildings 124
Value of Shade 125
Living Walls 126
Cooling Effect of Green Roofs 128
Green Roofs, Rainwater Attenuation and Cooling 129
Green Roofs Need the Right Substrate 130
Green Roofs for Biodiversity 130
London's Black Redstart Roofs 131
Biodiverse Green Roofs in North America 132
Roof Gardens for People 133
Worldwide Applications 133
Wildlife and Buildings 134
Rooftop Harvests 136

10. Conclusion   137
    Interesting Times   137
    The Positives   138
    Cities and Citizens Take the Initiative   138
    Greening Requires Greenery   140

Appendices
I: award winning projects from IHDC website   141
II: useful resources   177

Notes and References   197

Index   209

About the Author

Gary Grant is a Chartered Environmentalist, Member of the Institute of Ecology and Environmental Management, an Academician at the Academy of Urbanism, Member of the All Party Parliamentary Committee on Biodiversity, thesis supervisor at the Bartlett Faculty of the Built Environment, University College London, Chair of the Judges of the Integrated Habitats Design Competition and Director of the Green Roof Consultancy Ltd. After graduating from Nottingham University in 1980 with a degree in Biology, he worked for the London Wildlife Trust (LWT), campaigning for and managing urban wildspace. He conceived the London Wildlife Garden Centre which won a RIBA/ Times Award. Later he led the Wildlife in Docklands Project, a joint venture between the Wildfowl and Wetland Trust and LWT, which promoted nature as part of the redevelopment of London's Docklands. In the early 1990s, he participated in the Royal Fine Art Commission's River Thames Study and worked on the Natural History Museum's Wildlife Garden. Since the early 1990s he has designed green roofs, including the CUE Building at the Horniman Museum. Based in Hong Kong for the much of the 1990s, he worked on housing, tourism and infrastructure projects. In 2003, Gary wrote English Nature's Research Report on green roofs and followed that in 2006 with *Green Roofs and Facades* published by BRE Press. From 2006 to 2009 he was a Director of EDAW and then AECOM Design + Planning, where he worked on large-scale planning projects including the London 2012 Olympic Park, the Bedford Valley River Park, the Whitehill-Bordon Eco Town, Education City, Qatar and Saadiyat Island, Abu Dhabi.

Acknowledgement

Thanks to my friend and colleague, landscape architect Mark Loxton, for his role in the development of this project.

1. Introduction

I have an affection for a great city. I feel safe in the neighbourhood of man, and enjoy the sweet security of the streets

— Henry Wadsworth Longfellow

Modern Cities and the Disconnected

It may be unthinkable to many city dwellers, whether or not they enjoy the material abundance and culture or merely endure the pollution and stress, but life can go on without cities. Cities only became a reality, more than 6000 years ago, once agriculture had reached a stage where it produced enough surpluses to feed the required specialist workers, soldiers and bureaucrats. Until relatively recently in human history, before the rapid expansion in human population began after the Industrial Revolution, cities were relatively small, few in number and their impact on the natural world was limited. There had been human-induced extinctions of wildlife caused as hunter-gatherers mastered fire and spread into new continents, and early civilisations like that of Ancient Rome had caused widespread deforestation, but most of the natural world was still intact. People probably intuitively understood that they relied on the natural world, but seem to have always assumed that nature's apparently limitless bounty would be undiminished despite ever more exploitation. Much more recently, in the twentieth century, as the oil began to flow and populations grew

Ecosystem Services Come to Town: Greening Cities by Working with Nature, First Edition. Gary Grant.
© 2012 John Wiley & Sons, Ltd. Published 2012 by John Wiley & Sons, Ltd.

more rapidly, city people became increasingly disconnected from nature, so that nowadays many of us no longer understand how we are still ultimately reliant on the natural world for the goods and services that it provides. We have billions of environmentally illiterate people in our towns and cities who have little experience or knowledge of nature and have little appreciation or interest in what powers their lives, where their food or water originates or how their shelter, transportation or entertainment is provided and maintained. Some people I have encountered appear surprised, bemused or irritated when informed that their existence depends on the natural world. Notice how the mainstream television newsreader or newspaper journalist makes observations on nature, characterising it as little more than an amusing side issue, before returning to what are considered to be more serious matters of finance and politics. I appreciate that finance, politics and other cultural phenomena may shape the interrelationships between people but nature provides all the energy and the materials required for life. We must remind ourselves of this as we shape and manage our cities.

Population Spike

The relatively modest population growth (compared with that which followed) that was spurred by the early industrial revolution did not go unnoticed. Malthus published his *Essay on the Principle of Population* in 1798 in which he noted that the rise in population could lead to an increase in poverty and to food shortages.[1] Malthus published six editions of this work, and his ideas on population later influenced Charles Darwin's thinking on natural selection. As the number of cities grew and as those cities increased in size, forests were cleared and agriculture increased. Then at the beginning of the twentieth century, the oil age began. Fossil fuels (first coal and then oil) had freed people from a total reliance on energy provided by contemporary photosynthesis and allowed people to tap the energy trapped by photosynthesis and preserved in rocks through eons. With the new injection of energy and the food that came from this, city civilisation continued to flourish and even world wars did not bring any significant halt to growth. The population of the world grew from 1 billion in 1800 to 4 billion in 1970. It has now reached 7 billion and is predicted to peak somewhere around 9 billion later this century.[2] At the time of writing, global population is growing at 200,000 people per day – equivalent to another Reno, Nevada or Padua, Italy every day. Already more than half of the world's population lives in cities and it is highly likely that most people will continue to live in cities. We therefore need to consider how we can make life in those cities as efficient, comfortable and fulfilling as we can without continuing to rely on the unsustainable exploitation of natural resources.

It will not be straightforward and there will probably be no single solution, but the future will surely involve city greening. This book is intended to describe some of those difficulties and various ways that city greening can occur – not only for adornment and liveability, but also to make cities function in harmony with natural processes.

Limits to Growth

In 1972, the Club of Rome, an international think-tank concerned with a perceived lack of long-term thinking at the time, commissioned systems scientists at the Massachusetts Institute of Technology to undertake a study entitled *The Limits to Growth*.[3,4] This seminal work questioned the long-term viability of modern civilisation and identified some of the problems associated with exponential growth. It used a computer model to chart the interactions of five global factors: population, food production, industrial production, pollution and consumption of non-renewable natural resources. It was widely dismissed by contemporary commentators as an unsubstantiated doomsday prophecy, but along with an oil crisis, which followed in 1973, the report stimulated much thought and encouraged many activists and thinkers to found many of the conservation and environmental groups that emerged during that period.[5] During the 1960s, geologist M. King Hubbert had already explained that oil is a finite resource and described how production would peak – the so-called Peak Oil theory. This theory was also widely dismissed, even though production of oil had already peaked in the United States by 1970. However, the Peak Oil theory is now becoming respectable, with the International Energy Agency declaring in 2010, that production of global conventional crude oil had already peaked in 2006.[6] Some economists are now suggesting that the oil price rises of 2008 triggered the global financial crisis of that year and that the resource scarcity levels that cause the global economy to stutter – as predicted by the Club of Rome – are finally with us. Now some of the world's leading asset managers, led by Jeremy Grantham, are arguing that the growth in population coupled with increasing scarcity, means that the days of falling commodity prices are over.[7] This will eventually force the economists and politicians to face up to the likelihood that strong and continuous economic growth may never return and that a period of painful adjustment is upon us.

Global Threats

Even without the concerns over the depletion of oil, the acknowledgement (marked by the establishment of the Intergovernmental Panel on Climate Change in 1988) that the burning of fossil fuels has released greenhouse gases that are changing the global climate, began to change the way many people thought about our relationship with the environment.[8] A consensus emerged that environmental problems weren't just questions of localised and therefore avoidable degradation – they had become global. In parallel with concerns about fossil fuels and energy security, the second half of the twentieth century also saw a growing realisation that catastrophic losses in biodiversity were underway, with causes described by Edward O. Wilson and others as habitat destruction, invasive species, pollution and overharvesting – all exacerbated by population growth.[9] Although it is still not widely understood and appreciated by society at large, losses in biodiversity cause ecosystem collapse and reduce the capacity of the natural environment to provide the goods and services, including clean air and water and food, that we rely on. The United Nations Convention on Biodiversity, signed in 1992, marked the point where civilisation's dependence on biodiversity was, after years of campaigning on the part of scientists, officially acknowledged by our political leaders.[10]

Ecosystem Services and Stewardship

Now that there is an acknowledgement that our society, our civilisation and our cities are reliant on the goods and services supplied free of charge by the natural world – so-called ecosystem services – people are beginning to look differently at the way our towns and cities are designed, built and operated. This new approach goes beyond the necessary reduction in energy and water use and the mitigation of impacts to the wider environment. How mean-spirited it is to limit our ambitions to reducing negative environmental impacts! This new approach recognises that restoration of the natural environment will be necessary and that this can and should happen everywhere, in the forests, fields, wetlands, rivers and seas, but also in the urban environment. A substantial number of inspirational examples demonstrate that towns and cities do not need to be barren, hot and dry, they can be green and pleasant, with created habitats providing ecosystem services on and around the buildings where people live and work. This means that landscapes on and around our buildings and infrastructure can be more than an optional ornamental extra but a multi-functional layer of soil and vegetation that controls surface water, provides food and wildlife habitat and keeps us cool, fit and sane. To make this transformation from grey to green will require panoramic, trans-disciplinary thinking and coordinated action. We will need to move away from our over-specialisation and the widespread and common feeling that dealing with the conservation of nature is either irrelevant or in some cases, nice, but 'someone else's department'. We will need to think in longer timescales, in terms of ecosystems and networks, bio-geochemical cycles and chains of cause and effect rather than our nineteenth century, over-simplistic, reductionist and failing 'solve one pressing problem at a time' approach.

Greening Cities is Necessary

Cities occupy around 2% of the surface of the earth but now house more than 50% of the world's people. So to begin with, the greening of cities is important to those people. Cities are supported by farms, forests and oceans and the people who live and work in those places. Farms currently occupy around 40% of the surface of the land. Therefore the greening of cities is important to all those people too and has an impact on most of the land and the oceans. Of course, the greening of cities alone will not solve all of the world's ills; new approaches to agriculture, energy production, industry and natural resource management will be necessary, but in concert with all these changes, there must be a fundamental shift in the way we design and manage the built environment. This book outlines the beginning of civilisations and cities, because we need to understand how the process of urbanisation began and how it progressed in order to understand the present. There is an examination of the problems associated with urbanisation and the realisation, especially during the nineteenth and twentieth centuries, that these problems would require a coordinated response by state and local governments. There is also a look at the promulgation of planning and environmental laws and regulations and the development of policies, a process that became an international effort following World War II. The critically important issues of access and movement, energy and climate change and the natural environment, especially, water, soil, biodiversity and food are also briefly examined.

Hope

This book concludes with a hopeful look at how an understanding of ecology will change our approach to planning, architecture and landscape architecture, emphasising stewardship and restoration and working with the grain of nature, in contrast to the conventional approach which could be characterised as narrow, exploitative, destructive, dry, barren, grey and ultimately, doomed. Each city should be considered in terms of geological, climatological, hydrological processes and the biological region in which it sits. The intention is to be brief, informative, inspirational and practical. And optimistic – there is no benefit in being anything else. There is much more to learn than can be described in a few brief chapters, but there are plenty of references and links to help the reader to continue on the journey towards the greener city. Better cities will come with a new philosophy, which understands our place as part of nature, not as deluded creatures pretending to operate outside of it.

2. Origins of Cities

When tillage begins, other arts will follow. The farmers, therefore, are the founders of civilisation

– Daniel Webster

Why Look Back?

This book is primarily concerned with what I predict and hope will be a greener future for cities. It also describes some of the major problems and threats that modern city dwellers continue to face (see Chapter 4); however, like any phenomenon, cities cannot be fully appreciated without some understanding of their origins and growth. The purpose of this chapter is to give some insight into how towns and cities arose. It is useful to remind ourselves that city-centred civilisation is a recent phenomenon, that it is reliant on water, agriculture and transportation, is vulnerable to climate change, could be improved in terms of comfort and functionality and must be made compatible with the natural world. Civilisation is relatively new and we have much to learn and act upon if it is to persist.

Emergence of the Human Species

You are a human, a member of a species that has spent most of its 200,000 year history as a hunter-gatherer, living in simple shelters made from plants – a lifestyle that leaves relatively few traces, except

Ecosystem Services Come to Town: Greening Cities by Working with Nature,
First Edition. Gary Grant.
© 2012 John Wiley & Sons, Ltd. Published 2012 by John Wiley & Sons, Ltd.

for bones, shells, stone tools, hearths and the occasional rock painting or stone monument.[1] Nearly all of the timbers, tools and forest gardens of our forefathers have perished. Much of the environment that they lived in and their know-how have gone forever, making it difficult for us to reconstruct pictures of the past. During those millennia when *Homo sapiens* emerged on the African continent as one of several species of hominid, the use of tools and fire developed, but populations were sparse. According to the Toba catastrophe theory the human population collapsed to just a few thousand individuals around 71,000 years ago, following what volcanologists describe as a 'mega-colossal' volcanic eruption on the island of Sumatra, which probably darkened skies for years.[2] Once it had recovered from that bottleneck, the human population grew but probably did not exceed a million individuals until the invention of agriculture more than 60,000 years later.[3]

Great Leap Forward

According to Jared Diamond and others, around 50,000 years ago there was the Great Leap Forward, when people started to bury their dead, and make clothes, pottery and cave paintings. This was a time when culture really began to flourish.[4] Some humans also interbred with other species (Neanderthals and Denisovans) during this period, before spreading across the globe, reaching Patagonia at the tip of South America about 10,000 years ago and outlying parts of Oceania no more than a few hundred years ago.[5-7] Trade developed between Stone Age tribes, with pottery, tools and ornaments being relayed thousands of kilometres on well-trodden tracks across mountain ranges and by river and sea in dug-out canoes and reed boats. The hunter-gatherer way of life continued until the invention of agriculture and is still practised by a few remote tribes, but is now largely unknown and forgotten.

Agriculture and Permanent Settlements

Man was not the first species to harvest and store wild grains. Desert rodents do this and may have been observed by Stone Age peoples. The first evidence of people harvesting and storing grain comes from a time after a warming of the climate after the last Ice Age, which ended around 14,000 years ago. The ice sheets retreated in the north and then, around 12,900 years ago, there was a sudden interruption in the warming, known as the Younger Dryas, which lasted about 1300 years (see figure 2.1). This temporary cold spell brought drought in the Near East, which appears to have caused grassland habitats in that region to become more extensive. Archaeological excavations of a village of the Natufian culture, near the Dead Sea in Jordan, dated to

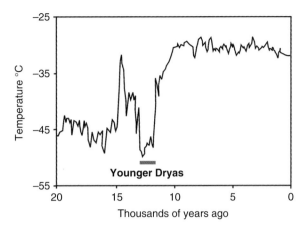

Figure 2.1 Graph based on Greenland ice core data shows how the climate suddenly cooled after a period of warming, around 12,900 years ago (the Younger Dryas), which led, perhaps, to the collection and storage of grain.

11,000 years ago, have revealed evidence of a 3 metres wide thatched roof and mud and stone granary with elevated floors that was designed to store barley and wheat through the winter.[8] This was a time before agriculture, when people collected and stored the seeds of wild grasses but were not cultivating them.

The move to cultivation was probably not a conscious decision but an accidental consequence of the earlier habit of collection, transport and storage, with spilt grain germinating and creating the first arable fields. We do not know exactly how it came about, but it is believed that the systematic cultivation of plants was first developed around 9500 years ago, during the so-called Neolithic Revolution, and this appears to have stimulated the establishment of more settlements where people could live close to their crops in order to be able to tend them and to collect and easily store the harvest in granaries. Çatalhöyük in modern day Çumra, near Konya, Anatolia, Turkey, was probably one of the first such settlements, starting from about 9500 years ago and abandoned about 2000 years later.[9] Up to 8000 people lived in mud brick houses crammed together on a mound overlooking a river and its floodplain (which was probably cultivated). There were no paths or streets, and access to each dwelling was via a ladder down through a rooftop opening (see figure 2.2). Waste was deposited around the margins of the settlement and the dead were buried beneath the floors. Containers were used to store wheat and barley, presumably to keep the grain dry and away from rodents and other pests. A similar settlement has been described from this period at Jericho, in the Jordan Valley. Although Jericho was smaller than Çatalhöyük, it included walls and towers as well as granaries and dwellings. Plants and animals domesticated at various times and in various places in

Figure 2.2 Çatalhöyük: one of the earliest towns and founded on agriculture.

the Near East during the early Neolithic include wheat, barley, lentil, chickpea, flax, sheep and goats. The agriculture of the Near East spread rapidly, crossing into Europe and Asia where many similar environments suitable for agriculture could be found along interconnected places, usually river valleys, at similar latitudes.

Agriculture Around the World

Agriculture was invented independently in several locations including sub-Saharan Africa, China, Papua and the Americas. For example, around 7000 years ago, the Yangshao culture, located in an area which lies within modern Henan, Shaanxi and Shanxi provinces in China, began to cultivate millet, rice and wheat and kept domesticated animals including chickens, pigs, sheep, goats, cattle and dogs. In sub-Saharan Africa agriculture began around 5000 years ago with the domestication of sorghum. Maize was first domesticated in Central America around the same time. Later potato, squash and sunflower were taken into cultivation in the Americas. The transition to an agricultural way of life was not always easy. Bad weather, including floods and drought, frequently led to crop failure; the ever-changing climate and the changing courses of rivers meant that villages, where people had invested time and energy into the construction of dwellings, granaries, wells and cisterns, could quickly become uninhabitable. Pathogens jumped from animals to people and spread rapidly through the new centres of population, where people often shared rooms with farm animals, and sanitation was usually poor. Famine blighted the lives of early farmers and people would often combine traditional hunting and foraging with farming, but over the centuries following the development of agriculture, forests were cleared, populations began to grow slowly but steadily, and knowledge of agriculture spread as people sought new lands to cultivate, usually in the larger river valleys or deltas where fertile sediments accumulate. Agriculture spread to the major river valleys in Africa, Asia and Europe, especially where floodplains tended to be inundated each year in a way that became predictable. Cattle were domesticated and pastoral societies became established on drier uplands so that trade developed between upland pastoralists and lowland agronomists, helping to stabilise economies and smooth out difficulties associated with bouts of poor weather.

Agriculture Intensifies

Around 8200 years ago, a large pulse of melt water from the disappearing Laurentian ice sheet in North America, breached an ice dam, entered the Atlantic and caused global cooling, a rapid rise in sea levels and an increased aridity in the Middle East. The drier climate seems to have intensified agricultural activity in river valleys and by 6700 years ago, had triggered the invention of irrigation by the Ubaid culture in Southern Mesopotamia.[10] Agriculture entered a new, more productive phase, which required more centralised control and which spurred population growth and, eventually, larger and more sophisticated settlements. Agricultural output reached sufficiently high levels to support more complex societies that began to build and defend large granaries and to develop systems of arithmetic and writing to account for the new-found wealth. These first cities became fortresses, ruled by self-appointed royal families and inhabited by priests, traders, weavers, potters and metalworkers – specialists who were no longer farmers themselves but relied on farmers to support them (as we still do today). Early cities controlled their agricultural hinterlands and became the marketplaces into which goods were brought, along the waterways and radiating networks of tracks. These first centres of wealth and power were characterised by monumental buildings (usually temples and palaces), paid for by taxation, built using manpower and all fuelled with grain. With their growing agricultural and trade surpluses, elites sought adornment and demonstrations of status, which in turn stimulated the growth of art, ritual, festivals and technical innovation. The need to maintain accounts and mark the seasons led to the development of writing, arithmetic and astronomy. The informal agreements moderated by tribal chiefs, as have been observed in Stone Age societies, were replaced in these new settlements by written regulations administered by officials loyal to, and paid for by, the ruling elite, a caste that usually represented itself as god-like. Climate change had stimulated the beginning of civilisation.

Empires Rise and Fall in Mesopotamia

In Mesopotamia (in the fertile floodplains of the rivers Tigris and Euphrates), the Bronze Age saw the growth of centres of wealth, based on agricultural surplus and the import of timber, stone and metals brought by sea-going reed boats and draught animals from distant lands, including Yemen, Anatolia and the Indus Valley.[11] The most powerful leaders were able to raise armies that eventually made the foundation of empires possible. Often cited as the world's first emperor is Sargon, whose lands were centred on the city of Akkad around 4300 years ago (2300 BC) and was probably created by the enforced merger of several independent city-states.[12] This civilisation was already benefitting from wheeled carts drawn by onagers (Asian asses) as shown on the Standard of Ur (an artefact consisting of mosaic panels from the Sumerian culture dating from 2600 BC).[13] It has been suggested that Sargon's role in directing the maintenance of irrigation ditches gave him control of a well-organised workforce, which subsequently became his army. This empire was reliant on both rain-fed and irrigated agriculture and when, after a hundred years, a prolonged drought struck, around 4200 years ago, it collapsed. After the drought that brought down Akkad had ended – a drought that lasted some three centuries – the Sumerian Renaissance began. The city of Ur (near modern Nasiriyah in Iraq) rose to become the largest settlement with an estimated 65,000 people in the period 2030–1980 BC.[14] Ur was the capital of ancient Sumeria, which also included the cities of Eridu and Uruk. Mud bricks were used to build two-storey villa homes, as well as other increasingly large structures including ziggurats (temples in the form of pyramidal structures with flat tops). Perimeter walls were constructed much later, presumably in response to increasing threats. During the course of the Sumerian Renaissance, there were problems with an increase in soil salinity, caused by heavy irrigation and high evaporation rates, and the cultivation of wheat was replaced by salt-tolerant barley. This appears to have caused a severe decline in population and the movement of people towards the north. Around 500 BC, when the river had changed its course and the estuary had been blocked by siltation, Ur was finally abandoned.

Nile Valley

Around 7500 years ago, a number of tribes had developed agriculture along the Nile Valley. Over the centuries people learnt how to cultivate and irrigate the floodplain, which generated agricultural surpluses.

Political power was gradually consolidated until 5150 years ago when the first of the dynastic pharaohs gained control of the whole of the Nile Valley. As farm surpluses and the population grew, the state was able to establish a literate elite who were able to mobilise and organise increasingly large numbers of workers, constructing tombs and monuments, most famously the Great Pyramid, built during the reign of Khufu (2589–2566 BC). Relatively little is known about the dwellings and settlements of ancient Egypt. Buildings were usually in the floodplain and made of mud brick, which has not survived as well as the masonry of tombs and monuments. There are, however, examples of towns built on grids and others that are more organic in layout, with mud brick construction used to create distinct residential, religious and fortified districts, typically housing 3000 people in sites that covered less than 10 hectares.[15] Along with the Akkadian civilisation in Mesopotamia, the Old Kingdom of Ancient Egypt collapsed 4200 years ago as the prolonged regional drought caused crop failures. Power was not centralised again for another 140 years, when the Middle Kingdom was established.

Indus Valley

From 5300 years ago until 3700 years ago the Indus Valley civilisation spawned the cities of Mohenjo-daro and Harappa in the Indus (and adjacent valleys) in modern-day Pakistan and India. Like those of the Nile and Mesopotamia, this civilisation also depended on the irrigation of crops in the floodplain. Farmers domesticated a wide range of crops including legumes, sesame seeds, mangoes and dates, as well as various animals including the water buffalo. Settlements were well planned and included communal wells, bath-houses and sewers. There is no evidence of palaces or temples, but the remains of large granaries and fortifications have been found. It has been suggested that the large walls may have acted as flood defences. Central precincts appear to have been planned but residential areas grew in a more haphazard, organic way as the population increased. Artefacts recovered from Harappa and Mohenjo-Daro (the latter had an estimated population of 40,000) include beautiful statues, jewellery and seals. Inscriptions are suggestive of a system of writing, although this is disputed. From 3800 years ago the region became colder and drier as the monsoon weakened and the ancient Saraswati River dried up. This may have led to the eventual collapse of this remarkable and, until recently, overlooked civilisation.[16]

Ancient China

Although they may have been preceded, the earliest described cities of ancient China are those of the Shang Dynasty, which was centred on the Yellow River Valley starting from 3600 years ago (between 1600 BC and 1046 BC). This civilisation is notable for its large-scale production of bronze artefacts, chariots and a system of writing. Yin Xu (near modern Anyang in Henan Province) was the last and most substantial capital city of the Shang Dynasty. Archaeologists have found a number of large rammed-earth foundations for palaces, religious and burial sites and workshops.[17] From 2300 years ago, major canal building, for both irrigation and transportation, was undertaken in the lowlands of China. By the 7th century AD the Grand Canal had been completed, making it possible for barges to travel between the Yellow River and the Yangtze River basins. Rice was conveyed from the south to support the political centres of the north. In the 10th century AD, the engineer Chiao Wei yo had perfected the pound lock on the Grand Canal, which made it possible for vessels, especially those carrying heavy building materials, to move easily both up and downstream. Previously, a mod-ified weir, known as a flash lock, had made it difficult for boats to move upstream, and passage downstream was often dangerous, so the pound lock, which didn't reach Europe until the 14th century, was a major advance. Canals made the establishment of remarkable cities like Zhouzhuang, in modern Jiangsu Province (see figure 2.3). When the Grand Canal was completed during the 7th century, Suzhou, the city famous for silk, found itself on a major trading route and became a centre of industry and commerce and, eventually, the birthplace of China's famous private gardens during the Ming dynasty (1368–1644). Despite being ransacked on many occasions over the centuries, Suzhou's strategic advantages meant that it was always rebuilt.

Ancient Greece

As agriculture spread into Europe from the Near East it provided the basis for the establishment of Greek civilisation, which started from around 2800 years ago, at the beginning of the Iron Age, and was centred on Greece and western parts of Anatolia. In Greece itself, although the land was well suited to the growing of olives and grapes, the steep hillsides soon lost their fertility through soil erosion.[18] Food shortages were common. This is likely to have been a cause of conflict and may have stimulated the colonisation of Anatolia, Sicily and Egypt, where grain was more plentiful. Progress in the development of ships was important – wooden galleys, with rows of oarsmen, which could travel against the prevailing wind and make progress during periods of calm, brought about a new era of trade and warfare. Forests were rapidly cleared and regrowth suppressed by increasingly large herds of goats, or were taken for charcoal. Shipbuilding relied on imported timber from Macedon, Thrace and Lebanon. Greek cities varied con-siderably in layout. Many of the older settlements had an irregular,

Figure 2.3 Zhouzhuang, Jiangsu Province, China – an ancient city founded on canals.

organic form, which followed the topography, but colonial cities were usually planned according to a rectilinear grid. According to Aristotle,[19] Hippodamus (407 BC) is said to have designed the towns of Piraeus in Greece, Alexandria in Egypt and Miletus in Anatolia in this way. These conurbations included two-storey, south-facing residential blocks connected via alleys to broad main streets and spacious public spaces. The Hippodamian grid is said to be the starting point for all planned Greek and Roman cities.

On the Ganges

Around 2500 years ago (490 BC) the city of Pataliputra (on the site of modern day Patna) was established on the banks of the Ganges. It was known to the Greeks[20] and became the most important city for a succession of dynasties for the next 1700 years and was probably the world's largest city during the time of Ashoka the Great (272–232 BC), a convert to Buddhism, who is still admired. Little is known about the city, but it covered more than 30 km² and was protected by a wooden (later masonry) perimeter wall and external ditch.

Rome

After growing for more than two centuries, by 100 BC (2100 years ago), Rome had a population of about a million people, rivaled only by Alexandria in Egypt. Cities of this size would not appear again until Constantinople (Rome's successor) in the 5th century AD, Chang'an (near modern Xi'an) in China in the 8th century AD or Baghdad, in the medieval period. The people of Rome were fed with the produce of North Africa and Sicily, which meant that they were vulnerable to interruptions of supply caused by bad weather and military conflict. The conurbation of Rome was the result of organic growth over a long period but places of worship, entertainment and public facilities were often carefully planned. Augustus, the first emperor (63 BC to 14 AD) instigated a major building programme, including the construction of temples, monuments and a forum. He was also responsible for improving the road and water supply infrastructure as well as the establishment of a fire brigade and a police service. Although there were earlier examples of long-distance roads, for example in the Persian Empire,[21] the first major network of paved roads was the 80,500 kilometres serving the Roman Empire (which eventually collapsed in 476 AD). The width of Roman roads was established by law at 2.45 m (8′) for straight sections of road and 4.9 m (16′) for curves, although actual constructed widths have been shown to vary, with some routes only 1.1 m (3′ 7″) wide.[22] The same legislation (the Law of the Twelve Tables) required an easement of 1.5 m (5′) around property boundaries to permit vehicular access. The width of earliest vehicles seems to have been determined by the width of two draft animals walking side by side (about 1.5 m or 5′). Pedestrians dominated roman towns – vehicles were banned from urban areas, except for government officials on business. Delivery vehicles were given night-time access only. Ancient cities were intimate in scale by modern standards, with relatively narrow streets and even narrower alleyways, but vistas did open up in the forum (town square) or amphitheatre. The Roman legacy is still felt today – dozens of modern European cities, including London and Paris, were founded during the Roman period.

The Moche

Wheels make a difference, but they are not essential – civilisations in the Americas never had wheeled vehicles and didn't have horses until after the Europeans brought them in the 15th century. The lack of wheels must have made life in the early Americas quieter and harder. Nevertheless, as Rome fell, the Moche civilisation in Peru, now famed for its beautiful ceramics and gold ornaments, was growing in power. It lasted for some 700 years from 100 to 800 AD and appears to have entered a period of terminal decline after 30 years of flooding followed by 30 years of drought, beginning with the climate changes believed to have been triggered by the 535–536 AD eruption of Krakatoa.[23] Moche agriculture relied on the diversion of river water from the Andes into networks of irrigation canals. Much of the adobe architecture from the dozens of Moche settlements has been reused or eroded, but one of their monumental adobe pyramids, the Huaca de la Luna, remains as evidence of their ambition, determination and wealth.

Mesoamerica

The catastrophic changes in climate, which began after the eruption of Krakatoa in 535 AD and caused chaos in Europe, also affected societies in Mesoamerica. Teotihuacan, for example, may have collapsed following warfare and famine triggered by drought. This city was the largest in the pre-Columbian Americas, inhabited by an estimated 200,000 people and included a number of stepped pyramids, tombs and temples aligned with a broad central avenue. It has been suggested that the rigid and precise grid layout of the city, in common with some others in Mesoamerica, is based on a seasonal celestial alignments, perhaps the sunrise on days of religious significance. Teotihuacan was a multi-ethnic city, and there were large residential areas with what were probably distinct districts for each ethnic group. Mayans were one of the ethnic groups represented at Teotihuacan but many of their own cities appear to have been built in a more organic way, following the local topography and integrating natural features. Mayan cities are associated with natural underground fresh water cisterns (cenotes) and there were causeways connecting plazas, and great buildings including temples, courts for ball games and palaces, but much of the remainder of their towns tended to be a sprawl consisting of the simple dwellings of ordinary people.

Fortified Centres of Administration

The cities of the ancient world were situated in fertile regions and continued to fulfil roles in trade and administration for centuries, even if the capitals were moved occasionally to suit particular dynasties. A common arrangement was to completely encircle a settlement with walls and ditches, usually beginning with earth and wood and later with masonry. Within the largest settlements there would be a fortified citadel enclosing the political and religious centre with a marketplace nearby. As cities grew, dwellings would spread outside of the city walls and this would occasionally necessitate the construction of outer walls. Fortifications could become virtually impenetrable, but of course cities are always vulnerable to prolonged siege, because they cannot grow enough food within their own boundaries, even if every yard and terrace were given over to the growing of fruit and vegetables (see Chapter 4). It is worth noting that nearly all ancient cities were small in comparison with their modern counterparts, with the wider countryside always in view, and rural life still familiar to everyone.

European Renaissance

During the European Renaissance, rulers began to consider the remodelling of cities to cope with crowds during festivals and on market days, to improve circulation and create a more pleasing outlook. Many of the great public spaces of Italian cities, for example the Piazza del Campo of Sienna, date from this era. The centres of

Figure 2.4 Modern aerial photo of Lucca – the ancient fortifications now serve as a green girdle.

ancient cities were often renewed to create squares and vistas along straightened and widened main thoroughfares. The development of powerful artillery during the medieval period meant that city walls (like those of Lucca, Italy – see figure 2.4) were enlarged and strengthened, and gun emplacements created to provide defenders with clear lines of fire. Town planning during this era has been revealed by the Spanish colonial town planning legislation of 1573, which required cities in the Americas and Philippines to be laid out according to a grid of streets with a central plaza and defensive walls.[24] Earlier medieval examples of an organised approach to establishing the bastides of south-west France, where hundreds of new towns were established during the 13th and 14th centuries. Loosely based on the Roman grid, a typical bastide town consists of a central market, surrounded by colonnades of shops and dense residential districts with narrow streets.[25]

Early Modern

European colonial expansion, the development of guns, mercantile capitalism, the expansion of slavery and the establishment of centrally controlled modern states in the early modern period led to the catastrophic spread of disease and the destruction of indigenous societies and cities (for example, the fall of the Aztec capital Tenochtitlan in 1521). This period coincides with the further concentration of wealth and the expansion of European capital cities with new brick and masonry palaces, formal parks, radial networks of streets and squares with monumental displays. Notable examples of this extravagance include the Versailles Palace[26] (established at the end of the 17th century) and St Petersburg,[27] Russia (in the 18th century). Impressive as they were, these grand schemes did not change the lives of ordinary people for the better and probably helped to increase the resentment that led to popular revolt and revolution. Most people still lived in timber buildings, and even monarchs lived without proper sanitation. Crowded cities with narrow streets and people living above their place of work were vulnerable to disease and fire. In 1665 an estimated 100,000 Londoners (about 15% of the population) died from the bubonic plague, caused by the bacterium *Yersinia pestis* and transmitted by rat-borne fleas. The crowded conditions had ensured that people had suffered occasional outbreaks of this disease for more than 300 years, since the original Black Death, which had arrived in Europe in 1347.[28] A year later, in September 1666, the crowded (and at this time dry) timber and thatch buildings allowed a fire in a bakery to grow into a firestorm, which destroyed much of the medieval city of London. Figure 2.5 shows Staple Inn, one of the few buildings from the period to survive to the present day. Christopher Wren and others

Figure 2.5 Staple Inn, a medieval London building dating from before the Great Fire.

had recently formed the Royal Society, an early scientific society (which is still thriving), and members were eager to apply their rational approach to the rebuilding.[29] Radical plans by Wren, Hooke and others to create a new city of avenues and piazzas were resisted by the city's merchants and so the capital was rebuilt along its original street alignments. There were major changes, however, with St Paul's Cathedral and churches rebuilt and enlarged, thoroughfares widened and masonry and brick replacing timber. The urban terrace was also popularised during this period, with several major developments in London by Nicholas Barbon (see figure 2.6). The management of the public realm also improved, with better street cleansing. Progress had been made, but at the turn of the 18th century, city dwellers did not have sewerage systems. Piped water supplies began, and microscopes were beginning to open up study of tiny objects, but people were unaware of the microbial agents that caused most disease. Printing, international trade and banking developed rapidly and chimneys

Figure 2.6 Seventeenth century brick and masonry London terrace – very different from the earlier, cramped timber and thatch structures, which preceded the Great Fire.

and glass became commonplace, but the majority of people still lived in conditions that would be recognisable to those who had lived centuries before.

Squalor

Cities in the 18th century were still relatively small. The largest cities in Europe had hundreds of thousands of inhabitants. London, one of the world's largest cities at the time, had three-quarters of a million inhabitants in 1760.[30] Streets were narrow and roads were often blocked with mud, manure or food waste, but the city limits and the market gardens and farms, which supported everyone, were within walking distance. There was a high reliance on the transportation of goods by water. Cities did not have parks, although the rich could enjoy walled gardens and royalty, private hunting preserves, often close to the town. Although sewage was not treated, rivers like London's Thames were yet to be overwhelmed by waste and still supported a variety of fish, including salmon. The quality of the environment would get much worse before there was a concerted effort to do something about it. In Chapter 3, I describe how the Industrial Revolution brought about a population explosion and the associated squalor and disease along with unprecedented changes in the urban fabric and transportation.

3. Modern Cities

Every time I see an adult on a bicycle, I no longer despair for the future of the human race

– H.G. Wells

Origins of the Modern City

Life in 18th century European cities began to change as the interest in science took root and the realisation that life can be improved led to advances in agriculture and transportation, the invention of steam-powered engines and the exploitation of coal. The questioning of religious fundamentalism and traditional thought, known as the Enlightenment, led to technological advances and population growth, but also provided the intellectual justification for violent struggles for political power, most notably the American Revolutionary War (1775–1783) and the French Revolution (1789–1799). These changes in thinking led to changes in the built environment.

Industrial Revolution

In Britain during the 18th century, a canal network was established, in the first instance, for the transportation of coal. This had a dramatic effect. Once Brindley's Bridgewater Canal was opened, the price of coal in the Manchester market was halved.[1] Although mechanisation had

Ecosystem Services Come to Town: Greening Cities by Working with Nature,
First Edition. Gary Grant.
© 2012 John Wiley & Sons, Ltd. Published 2012 by John Wiley & Sons, Ltd.

begun with water mills, it was the shift to cheap coal, the fuel powering steam engines and furnaces, which really underpinned the remarkable population growth and associated changes that continued throughout the 19th century. Agriculture also benefitted from better crop rotations and the mechanisation of ploughing, seeding and harvesting. The injection of fossil fuel energy in the form of cheap coal meant that the population of Britain climbed from 10 million in 1800 to 37 million in 1900. Although there was population growth and technological progress, there was also painful change and periods of famine in the early 19th century. Many folk, tormented by poverty, or forced from the land in the name of agricultural reform, left for a new life in North America and elsewhere. New York City, one of the centres of immigration, grew from 313,000 in 1840 to more than 3.4 million by 1900.[2]

Railways

The canals helped to begin the industrial revolution but they had limitations. They were expensive to construct, required large quantities of water and could not be taken across higher ground without locks or tunnels. This meant that railways replaced the canals as industry's main means of transportation very quickly – within a few decades. Railways accelerated the pace of industrialisation and also changed the face of cities. Steam locomotives running on metal rails reached commercial viability with the establishment of the Stockton and Darlington Railway in 1825.[3] At first, railways were largely operated for the movement of coal, raw materials and finished goods but the Liverpool and Manchester Railway, opened in 1830, proved that the transportation of people could also be a viable business. There was feverish investment in the expansion of railway networks everywhere. Much money was lost, but the legacy of the railway revolution is still with us. The width of the track in Britain had long been set at a relatively narrow 4 feet 8½ inches or 1435 mm (horse-drawn carts had pulled rail cars to and from mines for centuries past), but the necessity of stations that could process thousands of people, multiple tracks and the need for cuttings, viaducts and bridges, changed cities forever. In most small towns it was usually possible to build a railway station on the edge of the built-up area without inconveniencing the traveller or the townsfolk, but in London the construction of the major stations and track resulted in large-scale demolition and subsequent fragmentation of largely working class neighbourhoods. For example, Camden Town in north London was affected by the construction of the London and Birmingham Railway and Euston Station (opened in 1837), the Great Northern Railway's King's Cross station (opened in 1852) and the Midland Railway station at St Pancras (opened in 1868) – a total of three decades of disruption in a relatively small area. In contrast to

Figure 3.1 The deep and wide cutting at an open section of the (largely underground) Metropolitan Railway, opened in 1861. The works caused disruption for years.

Camden Town, the wealthy and influential landowners of Westminster, including the Duke of Westminster himself, were able to keep the railways away from the more fashionable districts.[4] The effect of this was to create a ring of termini around central London. Within this ring, horse-drawn traffic became even more congested than it had been, and this in turn triggered the development of the Metropolitan Railway connecting Paddington and King's Cross stations – the first underground railway in the world, which opened in 1863 (See figure 3.1).[5]

Rapid Growth

The railways did more than just change the appearance and form of existing cities – they helped to change the face of whole nations. Rural populations declined and the new industrial towns were established in coalfields or in places where raw materials, like iron ore, were abundant. Factories and homes grew up together. Mechanisation resulted in higher agricultural output, but farm jobs were lost and farm workers and their families often became homeless. Trade and commerce also grew rapidly, and country people poured into the major cities, usually to be exploited by slum landlords, who routinely housed several families in single dwellings.

Ill Health

There was little or no sanitation in the growing cities of the period. Faeces often contaminated wells and watercourses, and during the 1830s and 1840s large numbers of people died as the result of major outbreaks of cholera and typhoid. Piecemeal legislation followed and there was investment in water supply infrastructure, although this was not always matched with adequate sewerage and treatment (a problem that continues to this day). The poor health of the urban poor was widely believed at the time to be caused by bad smells (the Miasma Theory)[6] and this inspired the creation of well-drained and well-ventilated urban parks, where people could stroll, meet, relax and take in the picturesque views, away from the smoke of the city and the polluted wetlands of the city fringes. Park planting at the time was usually based on the ideas of John Claudius Loudon, a pioneer of landscape planning, who believed that marshes and dense undergrowth created dangerous 'miasmas'.[7] The first urban park was Victoria Park, in east London, opened in 1845. In the New World, after decades of campaigning, Central Park in New York City was created in 1857 (see figure 3.2). The park, which covers 341 hectares (843 acres), was laid out by American landscape architect Fredrick Law Olmsted and English architect Calvert Vaux, who won a design competition.[8] Sheep grazed in the park until 1934, when they were removed over fears that they would be taken for food by victims of the Great Depression. Olmstead had visited and been inspired by Birkenhead Park, in north-west England, the second urban park in the West, which was opened in 1847. In the same year, the germ theory of disease began to emerge, through the observations of the Hungarian obstetrician Ignaz Semmelweis in Vienna, who had introduced hand-washing to combat high-mortality rates at a maternity clinic.[9] A few years later, in 1854, John Snow traced the origins of a cholera outbreak in Soho, London, to a sewage-contaminated public water pump.[10] In Britain, the Public Heath Act, which was eventually passed in 1875, gave power to local authorities to provide public sewers, regulate housing standards and widen streets.[11] Momentous progress in the understanding of disease had occurred during the previous 25 years, but the link in the public mind between public parks and health had been weakened as the miasma theory faded away.

Figure 3.2 Central Park, New York City. Opened in 1863 after decades of campaigning.

Distinctive New Districts Emerge

Advances in transport, including shipping, meant that demolition and rebuilding in older cities was widespread. City centres continued to host major civic buildings and business headquarters, but these were often close to warehouses (especially in port cities) and factories, although the latter were often moved to the outskirts of cities as problems with industrial pollution became intolerable. Regulations were passed in cities in the Netherlands, Germany and England to protect residential areas by setting minimum building standards and moving particularly noxious industries to the outskirts. For example, the London Building Act 1844, drafted during a time when the miasma theory still held sway, set standards for drainage, chimneys and minimum street widths (40 feet or 12 metres) as well as relocating various noxious and 'deleterious' works to the outskirts of conurbations. The new urbanites sought entertainment and more sophisticated shopping, and so specialist districts became established to cater for these demands. Working people lived close to their places of employment, whilst the wealthy began to use the improving transportation infrastructure to commute to larger suburban homes with gardens, cleansed by the sweet fresh air of the countryside.

Figure 3.3 Tree lined Avenue de la Grande Armée, created by Baron Haussmann in the second half of the 19th century.

Paris Re-born

In 1853, Baron Haussmann was commissioned by Napoleon III to bring about a 'strategic beautification' of Paris.[12] Haussmann directed this project for two decades, until he was dismissed, but work continued until the end of the 19th century. Haussmann created Paris's tree-lined boulevards (see figure 3.3), parks, gardens and modern system of sewers and waterworks. Many of the narrow medieval streets and associated overcrowded housing areas with limited light and poor sanitation were removed. Although one intention was to prevent the recurrence of cholera epidemics (20,000 of Paris's population of 650,000 were killed by cholera in 1832), it has also been suggested that another objective was to create wider streets that would make riots easier to control. The clearances of medieval precincts also had negative consequences, with some breakdown of social cohesion as close-knit communities were often widely dispersed. Haussmann's scheme for Paris has had an influence on urban planners ever since.

Railways and Suburbs

An unintended impact of the railways was the creation of suburbs populated by middle-class commuters, eager to enjoy the combination of new dwellings and green space on offer at the end of a short train journey. Beginning in the 1850s, the citizens of Chicago began to use the Illinois Central Railroad to commute to work. The first suburb was Hyde Park, 10 kilometres south of the city centre. Within 30 years a star-shaped pattern of development, which depended for its existence on 15 commuter lines, had transformed the city and the way of life of its people.[13] By 1898, stops were even being added to the Illinois Central Line to allow access to golf clubs. In the major cities of Europe and North America, new waves of commuting, which benefitted a wider range of working people, involved the expansion of the underground railways (in the few places where these occurred) or, more usually, the creation of tram or streetcar systems (mechanised street-level railways) or elevated railways. These new city-wide affordable transportation systems brought workers to factories and made cross-town shopping and leisure trips possible. Although the earliest mechanised trams were steam driven, electrification began in the 1880s and, apart from a few oddities, was universal. By the 1890s, electric tram systems were popular throughout Europe and North America and as far afield as Bangkok, Thailand and Japan.

Planning and Zoning

At the turn of the 20th century, the beauty of Haussmann's Paris and other planned cities was widely admired, and the idea of comprehensive town planning, promoted by pioneers like Patrick Geddes, began to gain wider acceptance. An example of this approach was architect Daniel Burnham's plan for Chicago, which was prepared for a citizen's group in 1909. Although the plan focused on a series of improvements to the public realm, it was broadened to include the relatively new concept of zoning plans. This began a movement that eventually led to the Federal Standard City Planning Enabling Act of 1928.[14] Advances in building techniques in the 1880s, including the use of structural steel frames, made tall buildings increasingly popular from that time, particularly in Chicago and New York City. In New York City, the long shadow cast by the 36-storey Equitable Building had become a well-publicised cause for concern and this led to the creation by the city administration of a zoning scheme (the 1916 Zoning Resolution) to control the form and height of new buildings.[15]

Garden Cities

Ebenezer Howard founded the Garden Cities Association in 1899 (the forerunner of the still influential Town and Country Planning Association) and his book *To-Morrow: A Peaceful Path to Real Reform*, published in 1898 and reprinted as *Garden Cities of To-Morrow* in 1902, led to the garden city movement and eventually to the building of Letchworth Garden City and Welwyn Garden City, both to the north of London.[16,17] Howard's friendship with the architects Hermann Muthesius and Bruno Taut also resulted in the creation of Germany's first garden city, Hellerau, near Dresden, in 1909.[18] Howard had travelled to the USA and had witnessed the aftermath of the great fire of Chicago in 1871. He had seen Olmstead's plans for generously sized parks in Chicago and returned to England, inspired. He was determined to improve the health of citizens and eliminate overcrowding in industrialised areas by creating new settlements where the inhabitants would have easy access to a 'green belt' around the edge of the town as well as green space within the town, together with hospitals, libraries and shops (see figure 3.4). Employment areas would be located within the city thus reducing the need to commute, with many citizens having the options of walking, cycling or catching the tram (streetcar) to work. He envisaged a typical garden city as supporting a population of 32,000 and covering an area of 1000 acres (about 400 hectares).

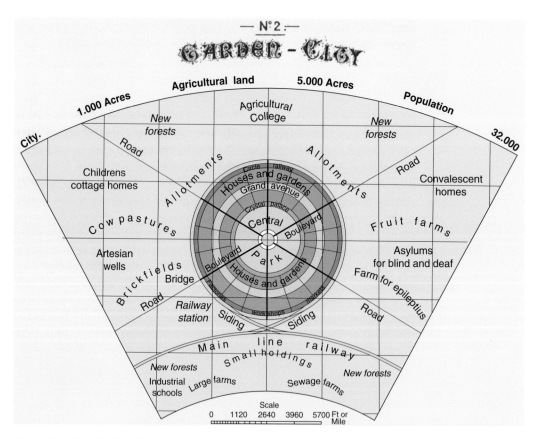

Figure 3.4 Graphic from Howard's *Garden Cities of To-Morrow* 1902.

Architects Barry Parker and Raymond Unwin won the competition to design Letchworth, which was the first garden city, constructed on 1600 hectares (3936 acres) of agricultural land in 1903.[19] Howard had advocated that land should be held in trust by cooperatives, with properties being leased and freeholds not sold outright, as eventually became the case. In Britain, such initiatives created an appetite for new legislation, with the Town Planning Act of 1909 requiring local authorities to prepare plans to regulate the number, type and location of buildings that would be permitted.[20]

Motor Vehicles Herald in the Oil Age

Karl Benz began to manufacture cars on a commercial basis in 1885, but it wasn't until the early years of the 20th century, after the commencement of mass production by Ford in the USA, that cars began to change the way cities operate, as railways had decades earlier. In 1906, London's General Cab Company brought 500 Renault motorised taxicabs, thereby bringing about a fivefold increase in the number of those vehicles on the city's streets. There was a similar switch from horse-drawn buses to motor buses at that time – between 1906 and 1908 the number of motor buses in London increased from 20 to 1000.[21] Motor vehicles were becoming more reliable, but were still outnumbered by horse-drawn vehicles until the 1920s when reductions in running costs took effect, largely because of the new more durable pneumatic tyres, replacing the solid rubber equivalents that gave a hard ride and wore down very quickly.

The trend for passengers to change from rail to road (both motor bus and private car) continued after the Great War (1914–1918). Few people missed the odour of horse manure as the numbers of horses dwindled, but, as the fleet of motor vehicles grew rapidly during the 1920s and 1930s, the public complained about choking clouds

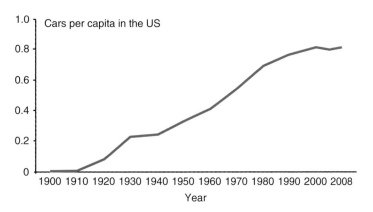

Figure 3.5 Growth of per-capita car ownership in the USA (after Litman 2011).[22]

of summer dust and the frequent collisions, resulting in deaths and injury. Reacting to these concerns, governments sealed most roads with asphalt (a mixture of crushed stone and bitumen – a product made from crude oil) and legislation was passed that required pedestrian crossings, road markings and signs. The surface drainage characteristics and average summer temperatures of many towns also must have changed significantly during this period, no doubt causing more flooding and damage to rivers and streams.

A Humane Outlook

One of the leading urban planning theorists of the period was the New Yorker Lewis Mumford.[23] He was an admirer of the garden city movement and argued against skyscraper cities. He could also see how the motor vehicle was beginning to change the scale of urban development, leading to the creation of urban sprawl in cities such as Los Angeles, where whole communities were developed to suit car owners, with anonymous suburbs linked into an ever-expanding road network. Mumford developed the concept of regional planning and sought to limit the size of cities so that they would maintain a 'humane outlook'.[24] He cofounded the Regional Planning Association of America and worked on two demonstration projects. The first was Sunnyside Gardens in Queens, New York, in 1924.[25]

Figure 3.6 Radburn, New Jersey was where the separation of pedestrians and motor vehicle traffic was pioneered in the 1930s. Here the footpath takes pedestrians safely under the highway.

This low-rise scheme was relatively compact, but contained gardens and central courtyards. The second project, which began in 1928, was Radburn, New Jersey. Consisting of 60 hectares of residential blocks with 9.35 hectares of green space (a standard of 15% of green space for the total site area). Schools were within walking distance of homes and the concept of pedestrian and vehicle segregation was also introduced (see figure 3.6). Currently there are 3100 people living in Radburn, which has continued to be popular with residents.[26]

Going Up

The extraordinary growth of Paris (which had gone from a population of 2 million in 1866 to 4 million by 1904) attracted the attention of Swiss architect Le Corbusier who, having realised that low-rise dwellings could never house rapidly expanding populations within the confines of existing cities, was interested in using the relatively new steel and concrete building techniques to build upwards. In 1925, in his *Plan Voisin*, he proposed clearing slums on the north bank of the River Seine and replacing them with high-rise towers set in parklands, in order to house three million people.[27] Although this was never adopted in Paris, because of the understandable public outcry, his ideas influenced a great many of the planning authorities in fast-growing cities across the world. Unfortunately, Corbusian schemes were often enacted without the accompanying parks and other infrastructure, which Le Corbusier had advocated as part of his comprehensive utopian approach. His 'machines for living' were well intentioned, but they took little account of local climate, hydrology, biodiversity or natural processes. If you would like to know what Paris would have looked like if Le Corbusier's scheme had not been rejected by Parisians, look at the contemporary high-rise housing estates of Hong Kong or Singapore, where expansion into low-rise and far-flung suburbs was not an option for the authorities of those hemmed-in city-states.

Continued Rise of the Motor Vehicle

Despite the best efforts of Mumford and the Regional Planning Association of America, the scale of urban areas began to change for the worse. The architect Frank Lloyd Wright, embraced the freedom offered by the motor car and proposed Broadacre, a city where every family would be able to drive to their own 4000 m² (0.98 acre) plot.[28] Although only ever fully realised in the most affluent of suburbs, this would become the model for thousands of towns and cities housing millions of people both in America and elsewhere. Plot sizes for homes and green space provision may not have grown, but road engineers

Figure 3.7 Modern suburb in England, designed with the private motor car in mind.

and city planners began to require multi-lane highways designed for speed, with wider streets, wider radii at junctions and land-hungry off-street parking. To explain the change in scale that occurred, compare a typical minimum street width in the contemporary United States of 16 metres (50 feet) with the ancient Roman minimum of 2.45 m (8 feet). Although it is not always an easy task, modern cars, at just under 2 m (6 feet) in width can still pass through most ancient thoroughfares. Another effect of the increasing reliance on roads was that shops, places of employment and schools were frequently located at considerable distances from residential districts, which meant that families learnt to make car trips for every need. Whole suburbs went without public transportation and no special facilities were provided for cyclists. Sprawling conurbations resulted in habitat loss and fragmentation, the culverting of watercourses and generic ornamental planting that lacked local distinctiveness.

Decline of the Inner City

After World War II, 'hub and wheel' road networks grew in concert with car ownership, and residential inner city areas began to decline as new cuttings, tunnels and elevated highways brought suburban commuters to the new office towers of the city centres, where significant

Figure 3.8 Sprawling Los Angeles – halted by mountains.

swathes of historic neighbourhoods had been destroyed or degraded. One example of this, amongst many, was Atlanta, Georgia, where three major highways converged on the heart of the city.[29] The highway networks and suburbs of adjacent cities brought about the creation of conjoined conurbations like Tokyo–Yokohama in Japan and New York City–New Jersey–Long Island in the United States. These metropolises became urban regions with multiple centres, with people crisscrossing by car to shop, get to work and be entertained. In many locations, further sprawl was prevented only by mountains, water bodies and, where designated, green belt.

New Towns

In 1937, the British Prime Minister, Neville Chamberlain, had become interested in regional planning and the garden city movement. He appointed a Royal Commission (the Barlow Commission), which recommended that housing and industry be moved away from London's inner-city slums to new towns. The objective was to improve living conditions and promote economic growth through construction and by increasing industrial output in the new well-connected factories. Legislation was passed (in the form of the New Towns Act of 1946) and several new towns, including Stevenage and Basildon, were

Figure 3.9 Burgess Park, south-east London, envisaged by Abercrombie 1943, opened in 1973 and still unfinished.

created. The idea of regional planning and the desire to establish new towns spread rapidly around the globe, so that by the 1960s, there were examples in many countries, including France and Japan.

City Plans

As the British New Towns were being conceived, Professor Sir Leslie Patrick Abercrombie was preparing a plan for the future of London. His County Plan of London (1943), better known as the Abercrombie Plan, assumed that people would move out from the overcrowded parts of inner London to the new towns and that new open space would be created within the most deprived areas of London.[30] After considering more generous possibilities, like the National Playing Fields Association's standard of 2.43 hectares (6 acres) of recreation space per thousand people (first recommended in 1938), he settled on what was considered a more realistic open space standard of 1.5 hectares (4 acres) per thousand people. Abercrombie was influenced by Frederick Law Olmsted, who designed a splendid chain of parks and waterways (known as the emerald necklace) around Boston, Massachusetts, and following this example sought to create linked chains of accessible playing fields, parks and allotments (vegetable gardens) joined together by greenways. Probably the most radical element of Abercrombie's plan was the creation of new strategic parks through the demolition of factories and slums, most notably the 46 hectares of built-up area in south-east London that became Burgess Park, which was eventually opened in 1973 but is still not complete.[31]

An Unfinished Task

As the 20th century ended, city engineers and planners in developed nations had learnt how make structures safe by introducing building standards, had provided lighting and power, brought piped potable water to people's homes and made provision for taking away foul water. Highway systems had been developed that allowed private motor vehicles and fire appliances to reach every door. After decades of decline, new investment was being made into public transport. Zoning had separated industry from residential areas and the huge new freight truck depots, shipping terminals and airports had (for the most part) been moved to out-of-town locations. Remarkable progress had been made in improving public health and increasing per capita incomes, but there were still concerns. Cities in developed countries were still unable to provide employment for all, and not everyone could attend a school in their own neighbourhood. 'Rustbelt' cities, where manufacturing industries had declined or vanished altogether, having been moved overseas to exploit cheaper labour, were run down, and crime and antisocial behaviour was still a concern. Standards had been set for the provision of open space, but these were often ignored by local authorities and there was increasing reliance on worn-out 19th century infrastructure (both green and grey). In addition, there were problems with surface water drainage, urban heat islands, air, noise and water pollution and the loss of biodiversity, which had never been tackled in any serious way at any time in the past. In the developing world, millions of people continued, and still continue, in places like Rio de Janeiro, Brazil and Nairobi, Kenya, to come to the city to begin new lives, often to find that the only accommodation is in informal settlements, without sanitation or paved roads, controlled by corrupt officials and criminal gangs – conditions reminiscent of early 19th century New York City or London. The next chapter looks in more detail at the problems, which continue to face our cities.

4. Issues Facing Contemporary Cities

Facts do not cease to exist because they are ignored

– Aldous Huxley

Impacts of Cities and City Living

We are advised not to focus on problems but instead to look for what works best – to work towards a vision for the future. This book is about how cities can be improved, and their wider environmental impact reduced, through greening, but before considering those essential improvements it may be useful to identify the negative impacts that cities and urban development have on the environment – impacts that should be avoided or mitigated. Cities and city living have a profound influence over local, regional and global environments and the ecosystem goods and services that the natural environment provides. Cities are also currently dependent on fossil fuels – this makes them unsustainable and vulnerable to price increases and eventually, shortages. The major categories of impact caused by urban development and city living are reviewed and, because this is an enormous field of study that cannot be described in full here, references and links are provided for those who would like to explore the topics in more detail.

Ecosystem Services Come to Town: Greening Cities by Working with Nature,
First Edition. Gary Grant.
© 2012 John Wiley & Sons, Ltd. Published 2012 by John Wiley & Sons, Ltd.

Habitat Loss

Modern urban development rarely takes place in wilderness areas. Usually new buildings and infrastructure spread onto agricultural hinterlands, where the natural vegetation will have already been removed or restricted to site boundaries, a process that may have occurred centuries ago. Nevertheless agricultural land retains some of the characteristics of the natural landscape that it once replaced. Species that favour open or disturbed habitats can thrive and where forest or other natural habitats have been cleared, elements of that original wilderness usually persist in the form of streams, field margins, woods and tree belts. These agricultural landscapes may have lost much of the biodiversity of the wilderness, but they still may have relatively healthy soils and watercourses and still provide a range of ecosystem goods and services. When urban development occurs on agricultural land, this leads to dramatic change (see Figure 4.1), although it may not always result in the clearance of all existing vegetation. This was often true in the distant past when countryside would become

Figure 4.1 Urban development results in habitat loss. Pictured is a suburb of Lagos, Nigeria, which is largely devoid of vegetation.

encapsulated by the growing town, perhaps because of ownership patterns or sometimes when deliberate efforts were made to create parks, first for the aristocracy (like London's Royal Parks which began as convenient hunting grounds) or for the public good, like New York's Central Park (see Chapter 3). Other open spaces in cities remain in the form of burial grounds or sports grounds or are incidental to watercourses or transportation routes. In town planning, there are deliberate efforts made to create parks and recreation grounds, but despite these efforts, urban development routinely leads to direct loss of habitats and species and the fragmentation of any habitats that remain.

Habitat Fragmentation

As MacArthur and Wilson described in their pioneering work on island biogeography, fragments of habitat differ from the original intact whole in several ways. Fragments are smaller and have more edge relative to the core and they may be isolated from other similar areas of habitat.[1] This has the effect of reducing the populations of plants and animals that live in the remaining fragments and brings about local extinctions. Disturbance and edge effects increase, which may benefit opportunistic and generalist species, but this creates unsuitable conditions for many vulnerable specialists that are associated with the more natural, pre-development environment. Species that roam freely across large territories and require large areas of pristine habitat for food, shelter or security, perish. Although some species, like many birds, may easily migrate to and colonise new sites, others are unable to cross what has become a hostile terrain for them. Preventing this isolation involves the protection of, or restoration of, connections between habitat fragments or a series of 'stepping stone' habitat patches for species (like some butterflies) which may be able to cross a limited stretch of inhospitable terrain (see Chapter 8 for discussions on the planning of ecological networks).

Impacts on Soil

Construction usually involves the removal of soil as deep excavations are made to prepare the foundations for buildings and infrastructure. Even in places where soil is still required following construction, existing soil is usually removed and replaced with generic manufactured topsoil, which may not be fit for purpose. Soil excavation and disturbance causes the decay of organic matter, which releases the greenhouse gas, carbon dioxide, into the atmosphere. Where soils are retained in their original location, they are usually compacted by vehicle traffic. Compaction reduces root penetration and may severely limit the soil's ability to store and drain water. Soils are also extremely vulnerable to erosion by wind and rain, especially during construction when they are denuded

Figure 4.2 Urban development (here an area in Perth, Western Australia) exposes soils to erosion by wind and rain.

of vegetation (see Figure 4.2). When construction sites are dry, they are usually shrouded in dust clouds. Following rainfall, sediments may be washed great distances, damaging rivers and even the marine environment. An example of where urban development has damaged the marine environment is where sediment smothers coral reefs, which may be close to the shore.[2] Erosion rates associated with construction are typically hundreds of times worse for any given area than losses caused by agriculture, reaching 55,000 tonnes per km^2 per year.[3] Urban soils are often contaminated with heavy metals and oils and are usually eutrophic (nutrient rich) which encourages colonisation by vigorous weeds or invasive non-native plants, which in turn stifles plant diversity. Probably the most serious impact that urban development has on soils, however, is the chronic drying effect that is caused by artificial drainage.

The Water Cycle

Cities have a profound effect on the water cycle. Rainwater usually runs off rapidly from buildings and streets into surface drains and thence into watercourses. This washes pollutants into rivers killing those species of aquatic wildlife that require clean water but it also creates strong pulses of water that can cause flooding downstream. Incidents of surface water flooding and the build-up of litter and noxious substances in towns has encouraged engineers to deepen and straighten channels, which usually has the effect of removing most of the natural features and dependent

Figure 4.3 Downpipes, piped drainage and channelisation of watercourses dries catchments, pollutes watercourses and causes downstream flooding.

wildlife. Piecemeal channelisation of river channels (which was commonplace during the 20th century) has usually exacerbated downstream flooding and sedimentation (see Figure 4.3). Where surface drains have connections to foul water sewers (so-called combined sewers), flash flooding caused by heavy rain sometimes causes sewage to enter rivers and streams, which depletes oxygen in the water and leads to fish kills. In London, in order to combat this kind of avoidable problem, Thames Water, the water company responsible for sewage treatment, can mobilise a special vessel, the *Thames Bubbler*, which can inject up to 10 tonnes of oxygen into the river per day.[4] Sewage overflows lead to the local extinction of aquatic wildlife. Potable (drinking quality) water is usually collected in reservoirs, extracted from groundwater or extracted from rivers, normally some distance away from the city, before sterilisation treatment is undertaken. Networks of pipes then deliver this water direct to homes and businesses. In this way, cities cause a drying and warming of the landscape and underground aquifers far beyond their boundaries.[5] Wastewater (sewage or black water from toilets and grey water from showers and sinks) leaves homes and businesses via sewers and is treated in sewage treatment plants, which are usually located downstream on the outskirts of conurbations. Not all sewage is treated, however: there are many cities that still discharge untreated effluent into rivers or the sea. For example, in 2010, despite the presence of three sewage treatment plants, Karachi, a city in Pakistan with 18.5 million inhabitants, was still sending an estimated 2000 cubic metres of raw sewage into coastal waters each day.[6] The prolonged drying of cities that occurs as the result of the removal of soil, the sealing of the ground and the networks of artificial drains, also changes the microclimate and is a major contributing factor in the reduction in humidity and the increase in temperature experienced by many cities.

Water-borne Pollution

Although most of the pollution of rivers has been attributed to the runoff from farms and industry, city storm-water runoff contains nitrates, phosphates and heavy metals from litter, garbage, vehicles, animal faeces, construction and open space management. Waters can also be polluted by increases in temperature (thermal pollution). Although the main cause of this latter category of pollution is the discharge into watercourses of cooling water from electricity-generating power plants, urban areas can increase river water temperatures through changes in water volumes and flows, general rises in temperature (see the urban heat island effect below) and the removal of tree shade from river banks. An example of thermal pollution to a river caused by a city is Long Island, New York, where water temperature was found to be elevated by 5–°8°C in summer.[7]

Urban Heat Islands

Cities have their own distinct climates and microclimates. Urban areas receive slightly less solar radiation than the surrounding countryside (because of dust and more cloud) but the preponderance of dark sealed surfaces and dense, thermally conductive materials (like asphalt, concrete and masonry), the lack of shade and reduced evapo-transpirative cooling means that radiation that strikes the city tends to be absorbed, stored as heat and reradiated at night. This domination by sealed surfaces and dense, dark building materials is the main cause of the urban heat island effect, which can result in a city like London being 9°C warmer than the surrounding countryside during a summer heat wave.[8] The highest temperatures are found at the urban core, and the urban heat island effect is more marked at night and when conditions are calm. There are some benefits – warmer temperatures in temperate cities means that they may be frost-free for three weeks longer than surrounding areas. The presence of buildings also creates a rough landscape that slows winds. Annual mean wind speeds in cities are usually lower than the surrounding countryside and strong gusts less frequent. Calm conditions are up to 20% more frequent in cities. Cities also tend to be less humid than surrounding areas even though they usually receive more rain each year.[9] The urban heat island effect has become a major concern for city governments. Summer heat waves cause more loss of life than any other weather related phenomenon and are made worse by the urban heat island effect. For example, the 1995

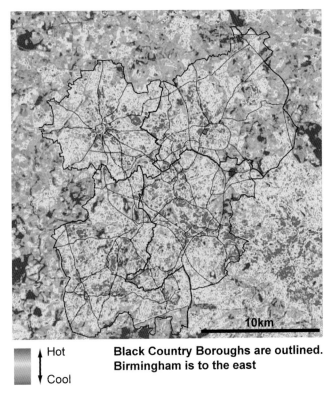

Hot

Cool

**Black Country Boroughs are outlined.
Birmingham is to the east**

Figure 4.4 Map shows urban heat islands associated with built-up areas in the West Midlands conurbation (Black Country and Birmingham), England.

Chicago heat wave resulted in 700 deaths and the 2003 heat wave in Europe resulted in the loss of 50,000 lives.[10] Climatologists are also predicting that in most places around the globe, summer heat waves will become more frequent and more intense as a result of climate change. For example, in the UK, climatologists are predicting warmer and wetter winters, hotter drier summers, sea level rise and more severe weather related events, including sudden heavy downpours.[11]

Air Pollution

The air around cities is polluted by emissions from motor vehicles, factories and power plants. Although pollution is often dispersed by wind, if the weather is calm, or the local topography is bowl-like, air pollution may build up. The main source of air pollution in most cities is now vehicular emissions. Pollutants include fine soot (particulates 0.1–25 micrometres in diameter) which cause respiratory disease and are carcinogens; sulphur dioxide (SO_2), which also causes respiratory problems and, following rain, produces an acid that damages masonry, vegetation and streams (acid rain); oxides of nitrogen (NOx), which also produce acid rain and react in strong sunlight to form peroxya-cetyl nitrate (PAN) which is irritating to the eyes and chest and is corrosive; carbon monoxide (which is toxic in high doses); lead, which reduces intelligence in children; other toxic chemicals including dioxins, which are carcinogenic; volatile organic compounds (VOCs) including methane and benzene (which is a carcinogen) and ground level ozone, which is a constituent of photochemical smog. The United Nations Environment Programme (UNEP) sets safe levels for air quality and provides a digest of air quality monitoring data for cities around the world. UNEP estimates that there are 1 million premature deaths each year caused by air pollution and the cost of air pollution has been esti-mated to be 2% of GDP in developed countries and 5% in developing countries.[12] In the cities of developed countries the trend has been for air quality to improve in recent decades as legislation is passed and various pollution abatement measures are adopted, but in the cities of some developing nations air quality continues to decline as vehicle ownership grows. Although air quality is improving in most developed nations, it is still a major public health issue. For example, the Los Angles area has seen a trend for continuous improvement since 1976, but federal safe levels for ozone are still being exceeded on more than 100 days each year.[13] Although the main thrust in air pollution abate-ment is to remove the source of pollutants by, for example, replacing diesel buses and delivery vans with electric vehicles, there is a growing body of evidence that shows how vegetation traps soot and absorbs many gaseous pollutants. In London, the government is now funding the planting of more trees and the establishment of living walls in order to reduce air pollution in especially badly affected locations.

Noise

Construction activities and transportation are the main causes of noise pollution in cities. Poor urban planning exacerbates the problem, for example when residential areas are sited close to airports, industrial areas or major roads. Excessive noise causes psychological stress and in extreme cases hearing loss, heart conditions and gastro-intestinal problems. Noise also has deleterious effects on wildlife, interfering with communication between individuals or preventing normal predator–prey interactions. Noise has also been shown to increase stress in mammals, even to the extent that it can limit the ability of an animal to find adequate food.[14] Regulations to limit noise pollution vary consid-erably from country to country and city to city and are absent from some jurisdictions. In the USA, following pioneering work in Portland, Oregon in the mid 1970s, typical sound limits in most cities are 55–65 dB in the day and 5 dB lower at night.[15] Again, vegetation and soil can protect people from excessive noise, with a standard 100 mm

Figure 4.5 Light pollution from excessive and poorly designed lighting obscures the night sky and disturbs nocturnal wildlife, such as bats.

deep extensive green roof, for example, able to reduce noise by up to 10 dBA, making this kind of installation ideal for protecting householders from traffic or aircraft noise.[16]

Light Pollution

Light pollution is caused by obtrusive artificial light, which is experienced in the form of a general glow or more localised glare from individual lights. Such pollution reduces our visibility of the night sky and is suspected to increase fatigue, anxiety and stress and is implicated as a causal factor in breast cancer.[17] Artificial light also has a negative impact on wildlife, disrupting the behaviour of birds, bats[18] and nocturnal insects (see Figure 4.5). Large numbers of birds are killed as they fly into illuminated buildings. For example, until lighting was modified in 1990, up to 1500 birds were killed each night by flying into Chicago's Hancock Center during migration.[19]

Agricultural Land Take

Cities also have indirect impacts on the environment through the demand for food, materials and energy. The area of farmland required to support a city dweller depends on diet. For a diet of grain or root vegetables, a single person can be supported by as little as 0.2 hectare (2000 m²) of agricultural land; however, for those with a richer diet

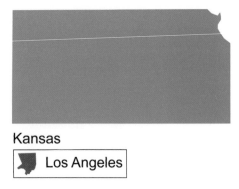

Kansas

Los Angeles

Figure 4.6 The area of agricultural land required to support Los Angeles is equivalent to an area the size of Kansas.

that involves frequent consumption of grazing animals like cattle, that per capita requirement increases to 1.4 hectares.[20] Assuming a requirement of 1.4 hectares per person, for a conurbation the size of greater Los Angeles, with a population of over 15 million, 21 million hectares (210,000 km^2) of farmland (an area this size of Kansas) is required (see Figure 4.6). Agriculture and food production also have a huge requirement for water. Globally, 70% of water abstracted from wells and rivers is used for irrigation. The global average water consumption for the production of a tonne of wheat is 1303 m^3 and for each tonne of beef 15497 m^3 of water is required.[21] Compare these figures with annual water consumption for personal use of 209 m^3 for an average American.[22]

Concrete

Cities also require raw materials, including cement (manufactured from limestone) and sands and gravels (which are components of concrete). Limestone and aggregate quarries do not take up particularly large tracts of land, and the land can be restored to agriculture or nature reserves, so the impact of the use of these materials in terms of habitat loss is limited, but cement production involves the use of high-temperature (900 °C) rotary kilns, which is energy intensive and releases carbon dioxide as limestone decomposes to form lime. Cement production requires approximately 6 million kilojoules per tonne – energy usually supplied by burning fossil fuel.[23] Cement production accounts for more than 5% of manmade global carbon dioxide output.

Steel

Another important material in modern cities is steel, which is used as a construction material and in vehicles and appliances. Iron ore mines are usually too large to be readily restored, so there is habitat loss associated with mining but the main impact of steel use is the high energy consumption and carbon dioxide production. Iron production is largely fuelled with coal although there is some limited, but increasing, use of natural gas. Iron and steel production is usually associated with land contamination and poor air quality. Despite advances in efficiency since the 1970s and markedly increased recycling of scrap, steel production remains energy intensive – the production of a tonne of steel in the USA requires approximately 12 million kilojoules of energy.[24]

Glass

Glass is another energy-hungry building material, the manufacture of which requires gas- or oil-fired furnaces operating at 1600 °C.[25] Glass production uses 3.96 million kilojoules of energy and releases 185 kilograms of CO_2 per tonne. Glass manufacture is noisy, and releases sulphur dioxide and oxides of nitrogen into the atmosphere. Large volumes of emulsified water are used in the process and this results in the production of polluted effluent, which requires treatment before being discharged from the factory.

Timber

In contrast to steel, concrete and glass, timber requires relatively little energy to prepare for market. The major impact of timber production has been the destruction of primary forest, which leads to catastrophic losses of biodiversity and the release of greenhouse gases as forest soils decompose. Although some (largely illegal) logging of primary forest continues, most timber is now sourced from responsibly managed forests or plantations, as certified by the Forest Stewardship Council, an independent organisation that promotes responsible management of the world's forests.[26] There are many other products used to make the fabric of the modern city, too many to consider here; however, good information is available on the energy required to manufacture, deliver and dispose of materials (and therefore their carbon footprint). [27]

Waste

Cities produce waste. In pre-industrial times waste was largely recycled, placed in local pits and hollows or, if biodegradable, spread onto agricultural fields, but in antiquity the largest cities did have organised waste disposal. For example, in Athens more than 2500 years ago it was decreed that municipal waste should be taken at least a mile beyond the city gates.[28] Following the rapid growth of cities during the Industrial Revolution, waste was collected by local authorities and dumped into river valleys, wetlands, natural hollows, quarries and even over sea cliffs (see the Glass Beach, near Fort Bragg, California[29]). When people became aware of the contamination of watercourses and groundwater from toxic wastes, legislation was passed, and sealed and managed landfill sites were established. In the UK, the Deposit of Poisonous Wastes Act was passed in 1971 after a public outcry when drums of cyanide were dumped at a former brickworks in Nuneaton. Similar well reported incidents in Germany, the USA and Japan around the same period provided the impetus for new legislation throughout the developed world.[30] In recent decades, there has been an increasing emphasis on recycling, supported by legislation. For example, in Hong Kong, following the introduction of a charging scheme, construction waste was reduced from 6560 tonnes per day in 2005 to 2660 tonnes per day in 2008. Nevertheless, cities continue to produce large volumes of waste, which is largely disposed of in landfill. In 2008, Hong Kong's daily per capita production of municipal waste was 1.35 kg, which amounts to 9450 tonnes per day for its 7 million citizens. Hong Kong is concerned that it is running out of space for landfill, with existing facilities expected to be full by 2015.[31] This is a situation that is repeated throughout the world, which is driving innovation in waste to energy schemes, composting, waste reduction and recycling.[32,33]

Drivers of Population Growth

So what has driven this extraordinary growth in population and the size of and number of cities? The Industrial Revolution, which began in England during the 18th century and quickly spread to Europe, North America and Japan, saw a transition towards machine-based manufacturing and steam power fuelled by coal. Mass production, the growth of factories and rapid economic growth led to migration from country to town. The population of England was steady at 6 million between 1700 and 1740, rose to 8.1 million by 1801 and by 1901 was 30.5 million. However, population growth during the Industrial Revolution was modest compared with the global changes that came about during the 20th century. In 1909 a German chemist, Fritz Haber, demonstrated how ammonia (a fertiliser obtained mainly from manure and guano at that time) could be synthesised from hydrogen and nitrogen. The engineer, Carl Bosch, overcame the engineering problems associated with the high temperatures and pressures required, and in 1913 commercial production of ammonia using the Haber–Bosch process began.[34] This marked the beginning of a new era for agriculture, with the availability of fertiliser limited only by the availability of affordable

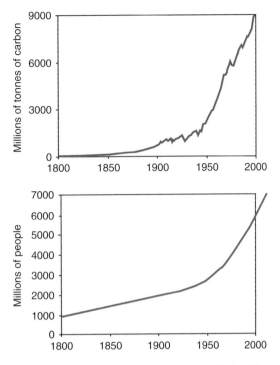

Figure 4.7 How world population has grown in concert with fossil fuel consumption.

energy. During the same period, oil was replacing coal as a more convenient and efficient fuel. In 1911, coal was still the primary fuel for the world's navies, but by 1919 all of them had converted their warships to run on oil, and the oil age had really got underway. The use of oil grew rapidly during the 20th century in concert with increases in fertiliser production, mechanised farming, agricultural output, motorised road transport and packaging. Conurbations grew in number, size and complexity. The area of forest and wetland dwindled, and the area of cultivated land expanded. There was a catastrophic loss of wilderness and decline in terrestrial and aquatic biodiversity.[35] Fisheries collapsed.[36] The global population increased from 1.6 billion in 1901 to 6 billion in 2000. This was the consequence of the availability of ammonia and cheap oil (see Figure 4.7). We are now dependent on oil and gas for our food supply.[37] Natural gas provides the raw material for our nitrogen fertilisers, oil powers tractors and farm machinery and food processing and delivery is reliant on oil. Without oil, it has been estimated that food production would fall by about 75%.

Modern civilisation has been fueled by oil, but the combustion of oil is a major source of increasing atmospheric carbon dioxide – a greenhouse gas that is causing climate change. The Intergovernmental Panel on Climate Change (IPCC) advises that even if greenhouse gas emissions are stabilised at 2000 levels, average global temperatures will reach 1.4 °C above pre-industrial levels by 2100.[38] A more likely scenario is that emissions are stabilised by 2025 with average global temperatures peaking in 2100 at 2.5 °C above pre-industrial levels. A 2.5 °C increase is predicted to result in reductions in ice caps, a sea level rise of 45 cm, stormier weather, more heat waves and more droughts. The scientific consensus is that some quantum of undesirable climate change is now inevitable. Steps should be taken to limit the change by switching to zero- and low-carbon energy sources (mitigation), but there is now growing interest in building resilience to climate change (adaptation).

Peak Oil

Oil is a finite resource. Peak oil is the half-way point of consumption, when the maximum rate of global oil extraction is reached, after which output falls and the costs of production progressively increase.[39] Oil exploitation for individual wells, whole countries or the whole world follows a spiked curve described by the geologist M. King Hubbert, who correctly predicted in 1956 that US oil production would peak between 1965 and 1970. Now there is a consensus amongst oilfield geologists that the global peak of oil production will occur between 2010 and 2020 (although many believe that peak oil has already passed). The United States Energy Information Administration predicts that global oil consumption will continue to rise from the 2008 level of 88 million barrels per day to 118 million barrels per day by 2030, with demand fuelled by population growth and increasing affluence in developing countries.[40] There are doubts, however, that the industry is capable of increasing production to those levels. The UN predicts that the global population will grow from 6.9 billion in 2010 to more than 8.2 billion by 2030 (an increase of 1.3 billion people – equivalent to 113 new cities the size of Rio de Janeiro, which has 11.5 million citizens).[41] There is much controversy regarding the likely effects of a decline in the production of oil during a period when demand is likely to grow, but the Hirsch Report commissioned by the US Department of Energy and published in 2005 concluded that peak oil will create an unprecedented challenge that will take an intense effort to find alternative sources of energy and that this transformation will take decades.[42]

Peak Phosphorus

Oil is not the only natural resource that is expected to become scarce in the coming years. Phosphorus is a nutrient that is essential to all life. Unlike nitrogen fertiliser, which is manufactured using the energy-intensive Haber–Bosch process, phosphorus is mined as phosphate rock, only available in a limited number of countries. The supply of phosphate is expected to last beyond supplies of oil, but it is predicted that, at present rates of population growth, phosphate mines will be exhausted sometime in the 21st century.[43] It is possible, however, to recover phosphate from sewage and manure (an approach that would also reduce pollution to the wider environment, notably watercourses, lakes and seas).

Post Oil

That concludes my brief review of the issues that modern civilisation faces. Given the seriousness of these problems, with the path to universal prosperity looking increasingly threatened, it is now of critical importance that these issues are addressed with a sense of urgency and vigour. To counter these threats, the post-petroleum cities of the future will need to include more soil, habitat and biodiversity. More food will be grown within cities. Cities will be water efficient and will collect rainwater, protect groundwater and maintain clean watercourses. Water and air quality will be improved and cities will be quieter, with more benign microclimates. More intelligent and subtle lighting will be the one of the most obvious manifestations of a new approach to the consumption of energy. Cities will generate some of their own power from sunlight and waste, and more journeys will be made on foot, by bicycle or on public transport. The intention in the chapters that follow is to describe some of the ways that these transformations can unfold.

5. Working with Nature

We cannot command Nature except by obeying her

– Francis Bacon

Ecology and Ecosystems

To work with nature requires some understanding of how nature works, an understanding of ecology. It could be argued that Charles Darwin[1] (1809–1882) or even Linnaeus[2] (1707–1778) were ecologists, concerned as they were with the economy of nature and the complex interrelationships between species and their environment. However, the term ecology wasn't coined until 1866 by the German biologist Haeckel, long after the Enlightenment and Industrial Revolution had popularised reductionism and a Newtonian, mechanistic, world view.[3] Ecology, therefore, was first conceived as a science some time after modern cities were established. Put another way, cities were conceived, and continue to be operated, in ways that indicate a widespread ignorance of ecology. An ecosystem consists of all the organisms in a particular area and the environment with which they interact, and although we often forget, cities are examples of environments in which organisms interact. The plant ecologists Arthur Clapham and Arthur Tansley, devised the term ecosystem in the 1930s and the concept was developed and put onto the academic syllabus by Eugene Odum in the 1950s.[4] In 1962, Rachel

Ecosystem Services Come to Town: Greening Cities by Working with Nature,
First Edition. Gary Grant.
© 2012 John Wiley & Sons, Ltd. Published 2012 by John Wiley & Sons, Ltd.

Carson published Silent Spring, which documented, for the first time, the impact that pesticides were having on the natural world, especially birds of prey.[5] This brought to the attention of a wide audience, the interconnections between human activity and wildlife. Many people began to appreciate that a short term, simplistic approach to environmental management causes more harm than good. Since the 1960s and 1970s, more than a century after the term ecology was first used, the ecosystem concept has slowly begun to change the way that people view the natural world, but the denizens of cities were set in their out-dated Victorian ways by that time. Therefore ecologically informed reform to the way we design, build and operate the built environment has been slow.

Born Free

During the post-war period, people began to accept the notion that wildlife and the natural environment have a right to exist and to challenge the idea, which was still prevalent in the 1950s, that the natural world and wildlife are provided solely for our entertainment or exploitation. Even fearsome predators should be allowed to live free, people began to argue – an alien concept to the average city slicker. This new mood was exemplified by Joy Adamson's book Born Free, published in 1960. Adamson topped the New York Times bestseller list, and her book was made into an Academy Award winning film in 1966. It is the story of an orphaned lion cub being raised in captivity and then rereleased into the wild, and this has continued to inspire conservation work ever since.[6]

Saving the Great Lakes

The Great Lakes, on the US–Canada border in eastern North America, cover 208,610 km² and hold 22% of the world's fresh water. During the 19th century these water bodies were the setting for the development of major cities including Milwaukee, Cleveland, Chicago, Detroit, Gary and Toronto, all receiving water from a huge catchment. By the second half of the 20th century, dams, deforestation, industrial-scale agriculture and the effluent from heavy industry had led to a collapse in the fishery and to poor water quality that was threatening human health. There was even a 'dead zone' in the relatively shallow Lake Erie. The sea lamprey is a pest species in the Great Lakes. It is parasitic fish which may have entered the Great Lakes through the Erie Canal, which opened in 1825, but it was not until after the opening of the Welland Canal in 1919 that it spread from Lake Ontario to Lake Erie, and then to Lake Michigan, Lake

■ Great Lakes Watershed

■ International Border

Figure 5.1 The Great Lakes straddle two nations and many states and provinces.

Huron and Lake Superior, where, by the 1940s, it had decimated indigenous lake trout populations, which in turn caused an explosion in other alien species on which the trout had preyed. Canada and the USA had signed a treaty on the Great Lakes in 1909, but it was the problem with the invasion of the sea lamprey, which spurred them into renewed action, culminating in the Great Lakes Water Quality Agreement in 1972.[7] The subsequent revision of the Lakes Water Quality Agreement in 1978 was of special interest because it recognised that the Great Lakes Basin (see Figure 5.1) was an ecosystem and that the restoration of water quality and fisheries is a problem that will require an ecosystem approach that emerges from research, cooperation and public participation. Here was the beginning of an official recognition that humans are an integral part of ecosystems and not separated from them. It is probably not a coincidence that the *Blue Marble* photograph of the whole earth, taken by the crew of Apollo 17 and the Club of Rome's Limits to Growth (see Chapter 1), both published in 1972, were beginning to change the way people thought about the world around that time.

Earth Summit, Ecosystem Assessment and Ecosystem Services

The ecosystem approach finally came of age with the United Nations Convention on Biological Diversity, a global legally binding treaty unveiled at the Earth Summit in Rio de Janeiro in 1992.[8] The ecosystem approach is the primary framework for action under the Convention, which is the key international agreement on sustainable development. During the 1990s many experts working in the field of conservation became frustrated at the lack of scientific assessment anticipated by the Convention on Biological Diversity. In response to this perceived lack of information, in 2001, the United Nations Environment Programme launched the Millennium Ecosystem Assessment, a four-year study, published in 2005, which described how human degradation of the natural environment was reducing its capacity to provide ecosystem services.[9] This introduced another new and powerful idea into policy discussions and project planning – the ecosystem services concept, which is a new way of explaining how humans are supported by and reliant on the natural environment (see Figure 5.2). These services include clean air, water, food and raw materials and have been classified by the Millennium Ecosystem Assessment into supporting services,

Figure 5.2 Ecosystem services (after UN Millennium Ecosystem Assessment).

provisioning services, regulating services and cultural services. Supporting services underpin the others. These are photosynthesis, soil formation, nutrient cycling and water cycling. Provisioning services include food, fibre, fuel, medicines, pharmaceuticals and fresh water. Regulating services are those that provide pollination, maintain air quality and climate and reduce hazards including erosion, flood, disease and pests. Finally cultural non-material ecosystem services provide cerebral, aesthetic and recreational experiences. Following on from the Millennium Ecosystem Assessment are various national and regional studies which are intended to describe the condition of ecosystems and provide an understanding of whether or not these ecosystems have sufficient capacity to continue to provide the services on which we depend. An example is the UK National Ecosystem Assessment, which reported in 2011.[10]

Cities as Part of the Biosphere

An ecologically informed approach changes the way that people design and manage the environment, including the urban environment. It recognises that resources are finite and that there are limits beyond which ecosystems may cease to be productive. This means that management of ecosystems needs to be planned for the long term. Short-term, short-sighted exploitation has been shown to lead to collapse. A notable example of this was the collapse in 1992 of the northern Atlantic cod fishery, which led to the loss of 35,000 jobs in Newfoundland.[11] The new approach means thinking and acting at all scales and recognising interconnections within and between ecosystems. Economists are now looking seriously at the valuation of all ecosystem services instead of, as they have done until recently, only the extracted goods for which there is an established market. For example, regulation of the water cycle or pollination have been assigned no value in the past, even though life as we know it would be impossible without these services. Compromises that are made in managing ecosystems need to be based on the best available evidence and should be transparent. This means that when citizens are involved in decision-making (as they should be of course) they can better understand the chains of consequence that may be associated with particular choices and activities.

Ecological Restoration

Another important concept that began to take hold in the 1980s is that of ecological restoration, the idea that it is possible to repair ecosystems, restore biodiversity and thereby boost the range and quantum of available ecosystem services.[12] Nature conservation began in the 19th century with the preservation of sites and the protection of charismatic species. Although that work was and continues to be an essential part of nature conservation, we now know that nature reserves cannot survive in isolation and need to form core sites within future networks of expanded habitats and restored landscapes.

Urban Wildlife

Cities are still sometimes considered as separate from nature. Of course they are ultimately supported by nature, even the most ecologically impoverished examples, but by bringing nature into the city, residents can enjoy, on their own doorsteps, some of the ecosystem services that nature provides. In the past these services have been restricted to cultural benefits – tranquillity and beauty alone. In addition, the simplification of urban landscapes (parks and gardens), inspired by the perceived need for the first park designers to protect people from disease-carrying 'miasma' also led to the loss of biodiversity (see Chapter 3). This loss of biodiversity in our cities eventually led to the establishment of urban nature conservation groups in the 1970s and 1980s, typified by the Urban Wildlife Group in the industrial West Midlands of England.[13] Dismissed initially by most other mainstream 'countryside' conservationists, who often considered city wildlife uninteresting or irrelevant, the urban wildlife enthusiasts are now part of the global family of conservationists.

Green Infrastructure

Cities need infrastructure to function. The term infrastructure brings to mind roads, sewers and utilities. Realising that green space is also an essential component of a comfortable city, planners in the USA and Europe now promote the idea of green infrastructure.[14] This stemmed from the pioneering work of McMahon[15] and others at the Conservation Fund who conceived the idea of state-wide greenways and then broadened the concept to become green infrastructure.[16] Green infrastructure takes green space planning beyond the preservation of a few selected sites or a minimum quantum of recreational space. There is a new emphasis on large-scale, forward planning of restored, interconnected landscapes. The concept emphasises the importance of multi-functionality, so that all sites provide a wide range of ecosystem services. It means that urban planning and design become less haphazard, with full consideration of existing landforms, biodiversity, flood management, water conservation, maintenance of microclimates and climate change adaptation as well as more traditional functions like recreation and relaxation.

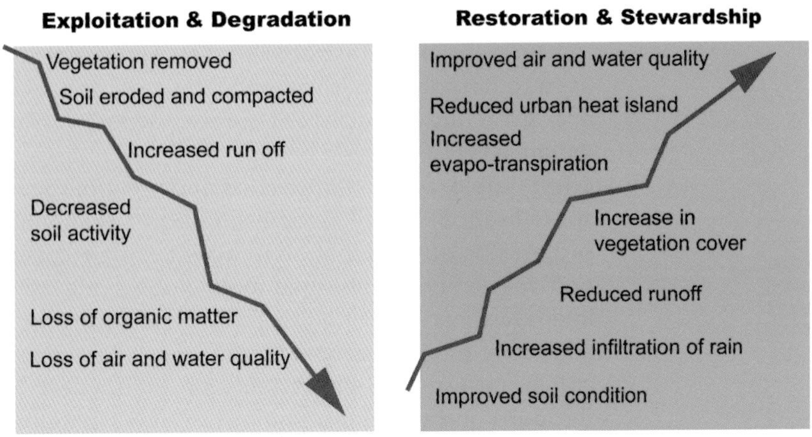

Exploitation & Degradation	**Restoration & Stewardship**

Vegetation removed
Soil eroded and compacted
Increased run off
Decreased soil activity
Loss of organic matter
Loss of air and water quality

Improved air and water quality
Reduced urban heat island
Increased evapo-transpiration
Increase in vegetation cover
Reduced runoff
Increased infiltration of rain
Improved soil condition

Figure 5.3 From exploitation to stewardship (after the Sustainable Sites Initiative).

Sustainable Sites Initiative

The ecological approach is now permeating into the design professions. In 2005, the American Society of Landscape Architects (ASLA) and partners launched the Sustainable Sites Initiative[17] which promotes a philosophy of land planning and design which recognises the need to create green infrastructure that provides ecosystem services (see Figure 5.3). Although the Initiative includes a way of measuring the worth of green infrastructure delivered as part of urban development, it has provided some invaluable guiding principles for practitioners, which are:

- Do no harm
- Use the precautionary principle
- Design with nature and culture
- Use a decision-making hierarchy of preservation, restoration and regeneration
- Provide regenerative systems as intergenerational equity
- Support a living process
- Use a systems thinking approach
- Use a collaborative and ethical approach
- Maintain integrity in leadership and research
- Instil a sense of stewardship

Advice from Professional Bodies and Others

The ASLA has blazed the trail for other built environment professionals and activists in other countries. For example, in 2008, the UK Town and Country Planning Association issued advice on green infrastructure in respect to eco-towns.[18] However, beware of confusion in the use of the term 'green infrastructure'. The expression is occasionally being used to describe improvements in the efficiency of grey infrastructure and even the financing of 'green' industry. The Sustainable Sites Initiative is also notable because it is described as an *inter-disciplinary* effort. The expansion of science and technology has led to increasing specialisation, where people undergo vocational training and enter professions or roles that often have a narrow focus defined by legislation, regulation, established technologies or a standardised approach. Interdisciplinary working usually involves people from distinctly different academic or professional backgrounds listening to each other and collaborating. This approach has led to new insights and breakthroughs and the establishment of new disciplines. Interdisciplinary working promotes innovation and multi-functional design through dialogue and mutual respect. Those of us who have promoted the universal importance of green infrastructure or ecosystem services will be familiar with the difficulties faced when dealing with specialists who feel that such issues are outside of their scope of work or irrelevant to their task. Clearly there is still progress to be made in engaging with the full range of professionals and academics, as well as the wider public, in the important task of greening cities. Interdisciplinary working, and knowledge of ecological principles, will help us to overcome these barriers.

Mimic Nature

Another powerful way of working with nature is to mimic nature. Biomimicry is an approach where careful studies are made of nature in order to develop new designs and processes.[19,20] This is not necessarily about copying but taking nature as a model, point of comparison or teacher. In using nature as a model, designers seek biological examples and then emulate these. An example of biomimicry in practice is buildings that emulate termite hills. Termites build mounds that maintain constant internal temperatures despite extreme exterior fluctuations in temperature associated with the tropical climate. Termites align their mounds to reduce solar gain, use the chimney effect, earth sheltering and exploit evaporative cooling through porous walls (see figure 5.4) and these processes are now being mimicked by architects and engineers in order to reduce energy consumption in buildings. A notable example of this approach is the Eastgate Centre in Harare, Zimbabwe, designed by the architect Mick Pearce and the engineers Arup Associates.[21]

Using nature as a benchmark can also be a part of an assessment of the sustainability of a design or process – evolution has tested certain life forms for eons. Biomimicry represents a new way of looking at

Figure 5.4 Termite hill, with natural internal climate control and the Eastgate Centre, Harare, Zimbabwe, that it inspired.

nature – not as something to be exploited or conquered but a source of inspiration and ideas. The Industrial Revolution took man-made systems away from nature. It made simple extractive, linear, wasteful and polluting processes commonplace. Our task is to replace these with interconnected, restorative, clean, closed-loop, zero-waste processes, driven by the sun, wind and tides.

Working with Nature Works

To conclude, working with nature acknowledges that humankind is part of nature. It involves the use of ecological knowledge and the ecosystem approach to seek new ways of designing and managing the built environment. Working with nature means thinking at all scales and using the whole catchment approach to bring about wise sustainable use of water and other natural resources. Cities rely on ecosystem services in the wider world, but it is important to remember that ecosystem services can be provided within the city by creating multi-functional, biodiverse, green infrastructure to complement (and wherever possible reduce or replace) grey infrastructure. Green infrastructure should be provided in the form of interconnected networks that make the city more permeable to both wildlife and people. This approach will make cities more resilient and better able to cope with climate change and the stresses that will emerge as civilisation makes the transition to the post-oil era. Working with nature will make cities more efficient and more pleasant. Working with nature is the only way of making our cities last.

6. Urban Nature

Will urban sprawl spread so far that most people lose all touch with nature?

– Frank N. Ikard

Open Space Preservation

Before the rapid growth in the size of our larger cities, brought about by the Industrial Revolution, people were rarely more than a short walk from the countryside. It seems unlikely that they would harbour the notion that they lacked contact with nature in the way that many of our contemporaries do. That changed as cities grew in size. Hampstead Heath, which is now within an inner London borough, was outside of the main conurbation of London until the 19th century. The area is mentioned in John Gerard's *Herball or Generall Historie of Plantes*, which was published in 1597. It continued to function as rough grazing land, and a source of sand and gravel, until part of it was secured for public use as natural open space in 1871. The preservation of Hampstead Heath finally occurred after decades of campaigning by people like Octavia Hill (cofounder of the Open Spaces Society in 1865 and the National Trust in 1895) and concerns over lack of access to green space for Londoners.[1] When the London County Council took charge of the site there was also a concern that the authority might turn the area into a municipal park, with the removal of wild vegetation. What is especially interesting about the struggle to save Hampstead

Ecosystem Services Come to Town: Greening Cities by Working with Nature,
First Edition. Gary Grant.
© 2012 John Wiley & Sons, Ltd. Published 2012 by John Wiley & Sons, Ltd.

Figure 6.1 Hampstead Heath today – heathland has become woodland but the site is still not 'park-like'.

Heath from development is that campaigners valued the wild vegetation and sought to maintain the 'judicious neglect', which had kept the rough heathland from becoming 'park-like'[2] (see figure 6.1).

The Naturalists

During the 19th century in England, there was a craze for the collection of fossils, flowers, insects, birds and their eggs. In 1858, the London Natural History Society was formed, one of many that still exist all over the country.[3] People scoured the countryside for specimens, which must have given them a understanding of, and appreciation for, what we now call biodiversity. However, the leading natural history writers of the time – people like Buckland and Wood – steered clear of Darwinism, perhaps because it was still controversial, so that the evolutionary perspective was often missing. The rapid loss of biodiversity that occurred during the 20th century was yet to get underway, which meant that conservation of species was yet to become a major concern.

Nature Leaves the City?

As the 20th century began and people became ever more mobile, the fight to preserve nature for public enjoyment moved from the

Figure 6.2 A typical contemporary urban 'cartoon' landscape of specimen tree and neat greensward – a legacy of both the 19th century desire to disperse harmful but imaginary miasmas and 20th century mechanisation.

town to the country. The Council for the Protection of Rural England was founded in 1925 and the issue of access to wild uplands for industrial workers of northern English towns came to a head with the mass trespass of Kinder Scout in 1932.[4] Amateur naturalists and the emerging academic ecologists seemed to have lost interest in cities by this time. There were exceptions, for example Max Nicholson's surveys of inner London birds in the 1920s, but as the 20th century progressed it seems that the idea that cities are not places to seek out or enjoy nature became the norm.[5] There was a continuing decline in biodiversity in cities, partly caused by air and water pollution and the removal of vegetation, but also by the simplification of maintenance of any remaining green space through ever more mechanisation. The rustic parks of the 19th century (Central Park was grazed by sheep until the 1930s, for example) were replaced by cartoon landscapes of lawns with scattered trees and water bodies incarcerated in concrete (see figure 6.2). In the mind of the average city dweller, urban nature had become absurd and irrelevant.

Urban Nature Returns

The movement against species-poor artificial landscapes is yet to win over everyone, but it began in mainland Europe where, for example, ecologists were involved in the creation of the Amsterdam Bos in the 1930s and continued with the restoration of city green space after the war. The abandoned and overgrown sites of bombed cities and the pioneer vegetation of abandoned industrial sites were also an inspiration to many of the pioneers of urban ecology, who could observe how wildlife can rapidly recolonise urban areas. Landscape architects like Ian McHarg, who wrote *Design with Nature* in 1969, began to promote the importance of ecology in landscape design and planning.[6] During the 1970s, the restoration of industrial sites and development of new towns (notably in the county of Cheshire) gave a small but growing number of ecologists and landscape architects in Britain the opportunity to experiment with naturalistic landscape planning and the provision of what we would now call green infrastructure. Also, during that period there was a new appreciation of the beauty and diversity of self-established vegetation on urban wasteland and its use by city dwellers, especially children, described by Richard Mabey in his 1973 book *The Unofficial Countryside*.[7] In 1975, Max Nicholson (the pioneering professional urban birdwatcher of the 1920s and first Director General of the British Government's Nature Conservancy in 1952) and landscape architect Lyndis Cole

Figure 6.3 An overgrown urban wasteland – still undervalued by most city dwellers.

wrote a paper entitled 'Urbanism in the Age of Ecology' which led to the creation of the William Curtis Ecological Park on a temporary truck park in central London close to Tower Bridge. In 1977, a number of habitats were created from scratch and wardens were provided to interpret the unusual scene to visiting school children, students, professionals and enthusiasts. Encouraged by practical projects like this and seminal accounts of the habitats of industrial areas like Bunny Teagle's *Endless Village* (1978), urban nature conservation charities began to establish themselves in the 1980s, with their work soon to be mirrored by new ecology posts in local government. One role for the new NGOs was to create urban nature reserves on wastelands – a difficult task when redevelopment was driven by both policy and commerce – and another was to bring wildlife back into sterile municipal green space. Although progress has been made on this latter task, the pace of change has been glacial and most municipal parks in Britain, 25 years later, still lack diversity of habitats and species.

Wildlife Gardens

During the early 1990s I worked on the design of the London Natural History Museum Wildlife Garden with my colleagues, landscape architect Mark Loxton and ecologist Denis Vickers. With leadership provided by one of the Museum's scientists, botanist Clive Jermy, an area of typical urban green space – close mown grass and the occasional flower bed – was transformed into a series of ponds, meadows and hedges, which are some of the typical habitats of the English countryside.[8] The scheme would not have been possible without the pioneering work undertaken at Max Nicholson's William Curtis Ecological Park (1977–1985) and the Camley Street Natural Park (which was established in 1984),[9] amongst others, but even in the 1990s the suggestion that species-rich habitats should be, or could be, created in inner London was still being questioned, even by some of the scientists working in the Natural History Museum. The Natural History Museum Wildlife Garden, however, has become an outdoor laboratory with thousands of species identified by the Museum's own experts (see Figure 6.4). The garden has also become an outdoor exhibit, with thousands of school children each year able to visit for a few hours to spot wild flowers and butterflies or enjoy pond dipping. Wildlife gardening has become more popular in the intervening years, with organisations like the National Wildlife Federation in the USA and The Wildlife Trusts and Royal Horticultural Society in the UK providing advice on how to attract even more wildlife to the garden.[10,11] There is also now further encouragement in the form of a significant body of peer-reviewed research, like that produced by the BUGS project at Sheffield University, which demonstrates that urban gardens are

Figure 6.4 London Natural History Museum Wildlife Garden.

surprisingly species-rich and certainly more biodiverse, area for area, than the typical intensively managed farm.[12]

Encapsulated Countryside

As fashions in landscape design have come and gone, cities have continued to harbour fragments of natural or semi-natural habitats. Often as conurbations have grown, patches of the former rural land-scape, so-called encapsulated countryside, have become encircled by urban development. These features frequently include boundary trees, hedgerows and ponds and small areas of grassland and woodland as well as watercourses. They have usually been modified and tend not to receive the traditional management associated with similar areas in the rural environment but remain as highly important habitats in the urban context. Some cities have grown up within areas that are recognised as global biodiversity hotspots. An example is that of Perth, Western

Figure 6.5 Urban bush land in Perth, Western Australia.

Australia, where there are a number of open spaces, which constitute isolated fragments of *Banksia* woodlands with many endemic species[13] (see figure 6.5). The encapsulated countryside of the Perth conurbation is particularly notable because of its location in a global biodiversity hotspot, but any remaining natural or semi-natural habitat which persists within urban areas, wherever it may be and even if it is relatively common in the region as a whole, form many of the core areas within actual or proposed urban ecological networks.

Bukit Timah

The relatively constant temperatures of the tropics are conditions that create more biodiversity than that found in the temperate zones. Singapore, which is close to the equator, is no exception. Although Singapore is mostly urban it supports about 2300 species of higher plants, roughly the same number as Poland (which has over 500 times the land area of Singapore). As Singapore developed, most of the primary rainforest was cleared, but a remaining fragment on high ground near the centre of the island, the 163 hectare Bukit Timah Nature Reserve, was officially protected in 1883.[14] Although the tiger and hornbills are long gone and there are fears about how indirect impacts like water table changes and disturbance are affecting the site, Bukit Timah still supports an impressive range of flora and fauna, with the forest canopy dominated by huge seraya (*Shorea curtsii*) trees. Following concerns about the negative ecological impacts that would be caused to the site through continuing isolation, a scheme to reconnect Bukit Timah to the adjacent Central Catchment Nature Reserve has been devised. It will involve the building of a 50 metre wide green bridge over a six-lane highway. The bridge will be planted with native trees and shrubs, in order to make it accessible for rainforest wildlife.[15]

The Urban Forest

Good citizens have been planting trees in cities for amenity and shade since the Enlightenment (and probably long before that). A notable example was John Evelyn, a member of the Royal Society, who encouraged tree-planting through his 1664 book Sylva.[16] Over time, widespread planting creates an urban forest – an ecologically impoverished forest without a true understorey or ground flora, but a forest in the sense that a canopy effect can be created. Now there is a growing realisation that the urban forest is more than good-looking and provides valuable ecosystem services including the cleaning of air, control of storm water and summer cooling. There are now easy ways of measuring the benefits provided by urban trees and the urban forest, with monetary values assigned – something that can help decision-makers to justify their commitment to investment in new planting.

Since 2006, the USDA Forest Service has revitalised interest in urban tree management with its i-Tree software suite, which helps city bureaucrats to put a credible monetary value on trees. To the credit of the Federal Government, this software is in the public domain, freely available and already in use throughout the world.[17] Typically tree officers choose new and replacement trees from a list of candidates species that are developed on the basis of appearance, minimum nuisance and proven ability to survive the urban conditions. Whilst these are important considerations, the challenge now is to develop a more sophisticated approach that considers other factors, including ecological value and the creation of green infrastructure networks. As more and more tree pits are designed to receive surface water runoff (part of the water-sensitive urban design philosophy – see Chapter 7) there will be opportunities to increase the range of trees planted in the urban environment, including trees that will be planted in combination with shrubs and ground flora in rain gardens.

Urban tree management is not easy – most cities have problems with large numbers of trees of a similar age, which mature and die together. It is therefore difficult to maintain a continuous canopy in the way a natural forest does, with young trees ready to exploit gaps as they emerge. There is also a serious lack of diversity in many cities, with an over-reliance on a small number of often non-native ornamental species. There are also concerns in cities with clay soils and older buildings with inadequate foundations (like London) where trees are commonly, but often incorrectly, blamed for causing or exacerbating subsidence.

Figure 6.6 The over-mature species-poor urban forest of central London. Vulnerable to disease and of low nature conservation value.

There are also many city-dwellers unhappy with the deposition onto their cars of sticky substances (honeydew) exuded from plant-sucking insects feeding on certain species of trees (for example trees of the *Tilia* genus). Despite these and other difficulties, there are many community groups and associations – such as the Alliance for Community Trees and the Tree Council – promoting the expansion of urban forests, with important partnerships developing between tree professionals and volunteers. The urban forest is a simple idea and affordable intervention that usually attracts widespread support and funding from both government and business. It is entry-level green infrastructure.[18,19]

Urban Wastelands

During the 1970s, as industry began to move from smaller to larger, cheaper, better-connected sites and from developed to developing countries, the vacant and neglected sites left behind began to flourish with self-established vegetation. The great variety of conditions in many abandoned sites – especially of the ground – gave rise to high biodiversity. Nutrient-poor substrates such as exposed subsoils or rock or imported industrial and building wastes support a wide range of wild flowers and invertebrates that are often rare in the wider environment. Where topsoil or high-nutrient spoils occur, rapid colonisation by tall herbs, scrub and trees make a contribution towards the urban forest. Often post-industrial sites support an intimate mosaic of vegetation types, adding to their interest. These remarkable landscapes, ignored for the most part by the average adult, became the haunt of generations of children, who would rather play in the informal setting of a vacant site than the sterile surroundings of the average purpose-built playground of the time. Although overlooked by the majority of conservationists, a small number of urban naturalists, including people like Richard Mabey, author of the *Unofficial Countryside*, began to appreciate that these sites were remarkable.

Canvey Wick

As the economy improved during the 1990s, many post-industrial sites in the West were redeveloped. Some remain, especially those where the cost and difficulty of decontamination of the soils makes redevelopment uneconomic without government assistance, but sites have been redeveloped for housing, retail parks and light industrial use. Where clean-up does take place, most techniques (with the exception of phytoremediation) necessitate the removal of vegetation and soil, which results in a total loss of ecological value.[20] Arguments that the vegetation and wildlife, or even the landscapes, of brownfield sites may be worthy of conservation usually fall on deaf ears, but there are exceptions. Canvey Wick, on Canvey Island on the Thames Estuary, was prepared for use as an oil refinery in the early 1970s, but the site was abandoned following the 1973 oil crisis. The area had been low-lying coastal grazing marsh but was filled with dredged silts, sands and gravels, and various roads and concrete foundations were constructed. Subsequently natural colonisation created dry grasslands and sandy banks, as well as various wetlands and scrub. These habitats came to support an impressive range of invertebrates, including rare solitary bees associated with natural river terrace gravels. As a brownfield (previously developed land in the UK definition), the site was originally earmarked for development but following meticulous survey work by entomologists and lobbying by the invertebrate conservation charity Buglife, the site was eventually designated as a Site of Special Scientific Interest (SSSI) by the Government's nature conservation agency in 2005 (see figure 6.7). This designation was a landmark because the site was a brownfield and government planning guidance prioritised the

Figure 6.7 Canvey Wick – a brownfield Site of Special Scientific Interest.

development of such sites. In addition, SSSIs were not usually desig-nated on the basis of their invertebrate interest, except for butterflies or dragonflies. At last, a brownfield site had been officially recognised for its importance for nature conservation.[21]

Emscher Park

The Ruhr, an industrial area in Germany, fell into decline during the latter part of the 20th century. Huge areas of industrial land became vacant, and realising that these areas could be re-zoned in order to create a new green infrastructure network, a consortium of 17 city authorities conceived the Emscher Landscape Park in the 1980s and opened it to the public in 1999.[22] It is a regional park 70 km in length and covering 320 km². The park was innovative in that its founders deliberately incorporated many of the derelict industrial installations and the rough vegetation that became established after abandonment

Figure 6.8 Emsher Park – Industrial installations and self-established vegetation retained.

(see figure 6.8). This is in contrast to the conventional approach to park construction, where all existing vegetation and soil is (usually unnecessarily) removed and replaced, often with a resulting loss in ecological value.

Urban Farming

There is a new enthusiasm for locally grown food, partly associated with the interest in cuisine and high-quality ingredients but also in terms of reducing our reliance of food shipped from afar and the associated carbon footprint. There is a realisation that large plots in the open countryside are not necessary to grow vegetables and that many crops are relatively easy to grow in all sorts of spaces including yards, balconies, window sills and roofs.[23] Once people get involved with growing their own food, they usually seek to cooperate with others, joining associations, swapping seed and produce and looking for ways of increasing their knowledge. Enthusiastic new urban growers, finding themselves at close quarters with soil and plants, are being increasingly drawn to an ecologically informed approach to cultivation, notably the permaculture movement. Although permaculture – a sustainable approach to settlement and agriculture modelled on ecological principles – is yet to have any significant influence on mainstream agriculture it has already found many enthusiasts in cities.[24] Agro-forestry ideas and practice will also influence the urban forest, with multi-functional fruit and nut trees planted instead of purely ornamental species. Plantations of nut trees are more productive than equivalent areas of arable crops and this has not gone unnoticed in Totnes, Devon, England, where volunteers have been planting almond, walnut, sweet chestnut and hazelnut trees in green spaces since 2008.[25] Another phenomenon is the interest in using vacant sites in post-industrial cities or even commercial buildings to establish large-scale farming in cities. Like many cities in the Rust Belt, Detroit has seen a loss of manufacturing jobs, city-centre population decline and the proliferation of derelict sites. One radical initiative has been that of Hantz Farms, which aims to create the world's largest urban farm, beginning with 28 hectares (70 acres) in Detroit's lower east side.[26]

Biodiversity Action Plans

The UK Government's response to the Convention on Biological Diversity, which was signed in 1992, was to establish a UK biodiversity action plan. Detailed descriptions of the country's habitats and species of conservation concern were compiled, and detailed plans were prepared for their protection.[27] Local biodiversity action plans included those prepared for individual cities or boroughs. Many have been written and forgotten, but some have been prepared to guide those who might otherwise have overlooked urban wildlife in their role as architects, engineers or contractors. I was fortunate to work on an example of this, the London Olympic Park Biodiversity Action Plan (BAP), which was required by the planning authority as a condition of their approval for the plans for the Olympic Park and associated facilities in east London.[28] The Olympic Park BAP took account of BAPs produced for London and the host boroughs. A target for the creation of a minimum of 45 hectares of habitat (including wetlands, woodland, species-rich grasslands and green roofs) of a certain quality was set and this guided designers working on buildings, parkland and the public realm. In addition, species action plans required habitats and features such as nesting or roosting sites to be provided for a range of species, including birds, reptiles, amphibians and invertebrates. Judging by some of the messages I have received, the targets have caused difficulties for some, especially those who have been used to creating conventional parks or buildings where the requirements of wildlife are ignored. As is being demonstrated, though, including habitats or features for species is not difficult once the commitment to do so is made. An example of a species targeted in the plan is the tumbling flower beetle, which breeds in dead wood. Log walls have been provided to benefit this and other

Figure 6.9 Log wall in the London Olympic Park, designed to benefit wintering and dead-wood-eating invertebrates.

species within the Olympic Park, evidence of interventions, which would probably not have occurred without the guidance of the BAP (see figure 6.9).

River Corridors

As cities have grown, often the remaining major open spaces have been those associated with river corridors, especially those larger watercourses that are too wide or wild to channel or build over. Waterborne commerce, which requires quays and warehouses, had often resulted in the removal of natural features, but even where these have been removed (as facilities have fallen into disuse) retained accessible riverside open space has usually been hard and grey. Urban riverside parks may contain the familiar trees and, occasionally, lawns of urban parks, but such areas are invariably disconnected from the river proper by vertical walls of sheet piling or concrete. Current thinking does encourage the consideration of softening urban river banks, but concerns over flood management and cost often result in the most radical proposals, especially schemes for the larger rivers, being dropped in favour of more conventional promenades. Despite difficulties associated with urban river restoration and the quality of green space, river corridors continue to be the focus for much urban regeneration and to function as important places for people to spend their leisure time.

London's South Bank

Areas that had suffered wartime damage and industrial decline on the south bank of the Thames near Waterloo Station were used for the Festival of Britain in 1951. Subsequently an internationally important complex of theatres and concert halls was established where pedestrians could enjoy a new tree-lined promenade.[29] These riverside public areas became increasingly popular as new pedestrian crossings of the Thames were provided and new attractions like the new Globe Theatre and Tate Modern were added within walking distance at Bankside.[30] The central London Jubilee Walkway was established in 1977, including a riverside walk that connects the whole of the south bank between Lambeth Bridge and Tower Bridge. The opening up of pedestrian routes along the Thames has certainly stimulated the regeneration of run-down areas, but the provision of wildlife habitats, ecosystem services and the potential to create wider green infrastructure networks (which is considered in the next chapter) had been almost entirely overlooked.

Minneapolis Riverfront

Now, in the 21st century, urban regeneration based on riverside improvements does increasingly include programmes for ecological and watershed restoration as demonstrated by initiatives like the Minneapolis Riverfront Development. This scheme, which considers the regeneration of an 8.8 kilometres (5.5 miles) urban reach of the Mississippi, will seek to improve the river for wildlife and make connections with tributaries restored from storm water drains. As well as economic regeneration and access and scenic improvements, the Minneapolis Park and Recreation Board has brought interventions to improve water quality to the fore.[31]

7. Water and Cities

Thanks to this hydrological cycle, fresh water is renewable, but it is also finite. There is a limited quantity to share – with each other and with nature

– Sandra Postel

Fresh Clean Water – Essential and Increasingly Scarce

It seems absurd to say it, but water is irreplaceable. Unlike oil or any particular foodstuff, it cannot be substituted for an alternative material. Life depends on water, and humans and many other species require clean, fresh water in order to survive. Although water sometimes appears to be abundant, especially when standing on the ocean shore and looking out across the blue, only 3% of the world's water is fresh (about 35 million cubic kilometres).[1] Much of this is locked up in glaciers (about 69%). The remaining liquid freshwater is found under the ground, or on the surface in lakes, rivers or in wetlands. This water is not evenly spread. For example, approximately 20% of the world's unfrozen freshwater is contained in a single water body – Siberia's Lake Baikal.[2] This uneven pattern of distribution means that relatively little of the world's freshwater is readily available for human consumption. As the world population has increased, so freshwater has become ever more scarce and it is also being increasingly contaminated with sewage, agricultural runoff and industrial pollution. Many of the world's major cities, including Beijing, Buenos Aires, Dakar, Lima and Mexico

Ecosystem Services Come to Town: Greening Cities by Working with Nature, First Edition. Gary Grant.
© 2012 John Wiley & Sons, Ltd. Published 2012 by John Wiley & Sons, Ltd.

City depend on water from underground aquifers, none of which are being recharged quickly enough to match rates of abstraction.

Civilisation has Modified the Water Cycle

The water cycle involves the perpetual movement of water through the atmosphere, with evaporation from sea and land, precipitation, storage in ice and snow, lakes and in the ground and surface flows. However, the amount of water which remains close to where it is consumed, has been significantly changed by human activity. Modern cities and their supporting agriculture modify the water cycle, through the drying of the landscape by abstraction, artificial drainage and the removal of soils and vegetation. This in turn reduces evaporation and evapo-transpiration. In effect civilisation, as currently practised, causes a long-term drying of whole landscapes, even without the effects of man-made climate change, which are predicted to exacerbate the problem. Added to this are the hazards associated with water-borne pollution, affecting watercourses (including those that supply drinking water) as well as estuaries and the sea. The United Nations Environment Programme predicts that by 2025 two out of every three people in the world will be living in conditions of water stress.[3] In addition to the problems of landscapes drying out through artificial drainage, climate change is predicted to cause summer droughts in many regions, reducing the rate of replenishment of reservoirs and aquifers and further increasing demand for water for irrigation.

Water Consumption

Per capita water consumption varies considerably across the globe, with people in some of the poorest African countries managing with as little as 30 litres per day compared with an average person in the USA using more than 500 litres per day.[4] Currently each citizen in Britain consumes an average of 150 litres per day, a rate of consumption that has tripled since 1950. This figure does not include water used in food production and processing. Piped water in developed countries is treated to high standards in order to ensure that it is safe to drink, but much of it is used wastefully. For example, about a third of potable water in developed countries is used for flushing toilets.

Embodied Carbon

There is another concern with water supplies – that of embodied carbon. Although the issue is not fully understood, it is significant. Water-related energy use in the USA is estimated to account for around 5% of total greenhouse gas emissions.[5] When reservoirs, water treatment plants and pipelines are constructed, there are carbon emissions associated with building materials such as steel and concrete but there are also carbon emissions generated by operational activities, most notably as water is pumped and treated. The amount of fossil fuel energy used to provide potable water can vary considerably from city to city depending on the terrain. In England, clean water is reported to have an average of approximately 0.3 tonne CO_2-equivalent per million litres (tCO_2e/Ml) of embodied energy. For wastewater treatment, energy-hungry processes are even more prevalent, especially where treatment must meet stringent discharge water quality standards. Again, in England, the embodied carbon in water averages approximately 0.7 tCO_2e/Ml. Therefore in England the embodied energy of water from when it is abstracted and returned after treatment is around 1.0 tCO_2e/Ml.[6] Australian cities are reported to have figures for embodied carbon of water of between 1.1 and 2.84 tCO_2e/Ml.[7] These figures are predicted to increase considerably where cities turn to desalination, a process that requires expensive infrastructure and is energy intensive. The conclusion is that water consumption uses energy and this in turn contributes to greenhouse gas emissions. Reducing water consumption will reduce greenhouse gas emissions as well as protecting the watercourses, lakes and aquifers from where water is extracted.

Virtual Water

Cities import food and products from afar and many of these materials have been produced using large quantities of water. For example each kilogram of supermarket food has been produced using several thousand litres of water. Industrial products require even more water during manufacture – for example motor vehicle manufacturers use several hundred thousand litres of water to produce each vehicle.[8] Such indirect water consumption is known as virtual, embedded or embodied water since the water is used at the place of origin or manufacture and not the place of consumption. Virtual water is a particularly important concept in understanding the reliance of population centres on imported goods with high-embedded water. Such goods can have a deleterious effect on the water resources and water quality in the region of origin. One of the most notorious examples of this is the Aral Sea, which shrank to a fraction of its original size as the rivers that feed it were diverted from the early 1960s to irrigate cotton farms in Uzbekistan. The drying of the Aral Sea destroyed the fishing industry, created employment and respiratory health problems. Although steps are now being taken to restore part of the northern part of the Aral Sea through the construction of a dam, this episode remains one of the worst environmental disasters of the 20th century.[9]

Catchment Management

Population growth and climate change are likely to trigger water crises in the world's conurbations, and new approaches are called for. One of these is integrated catchment (river basin) management.[10] Most of the rain falling within a single river basin or catchment will drain into a single point at the exit of the basin, usually a river, reservoir, lake, estuary or the sea. Water quality in the receiving body and flooding within the catchment depends largely on activities within the catchment. Therefore it makes good sense to integrate and coordinate the management of land use and activities within individual catchments. Where catchments are crossed by political boundaries, this may require special agreements (see Saving the Great Lakes in Chapter 5). Catchment management plans describe conditions within a catchment, including climate, topography, geology, soils and vegetation, identify sensitive areas and causes of flooding and water quality problems. Taking account of government policies, plans and standards, the catchment management plan then presents various options for slowing down and cleaning runoff which can involve limiting damaging operations or restoring natural features to the landscape. Working at a catchment level can help environmental managers to prioritise interventions. For example, relatively narrow buffer strips of natural vegetation can help to protect streams from sediments and nutrients, which can be washed from arable fields during heavy rain.[11] Management that is coordinated at the catchment level can also help people to appreciate the value of cooperation with others within the catchment and avoid the adoption of short-term locally initiated solutions, which merely send the problem downstream for others to deal with.

Rainwater Harvesting

Rainwater can be easily collected from roofs and other sealed surfaces. Even where roofs are vegetated, water can still be collected, albeit in reduced quantities (see the description of the Potsdamer Platz below). Although rainwater can be harvested for drinking, as it passes across a roof it can become contaminated with heavy metals or pathogens and would normally require treatment before it is consumed. Some jurisdictions place strict controls on harvesting rainwater for drinking, but it is usually a straightforward procedure to harvest rainwater for flushing toilets, washing clothes or irrigating plants. Harvested rainwater is usually stored in tanks in order to prevent contamination or colonisation by weed or mosquitoes; however, it may be used to recharge groundwater or feed rain gardens, open wells, ponds or reservoirs. The most important and costly component of a typical rainwater harvesting system is the storage tank, which must be sized to allow demands to be met through any dry periods. Standards and practice for rainwater harvesting are somewhat variable around the world and this prompted sustainable development leaders to establish the International Rainwater Harvesting Alliance in 2002.[12]

Grey Water

More than half of the water used in a typical home is used for bathing and washing. When it enters the drains it is known as grey water.[13] It is contaminated with soaps, detergents, grease and hair and some microbes. It usually enters the foul water sewers along with sewage (black water) to be treated at the district sewage treatment plant; however, grey water can be easily treated on site, providing water that is suitable for toilet flushing, washing clothes or irrigation. Grey water can be treated in wetland treatment systems (including wetland roofs or living walls) or more usually, compact filtration vessels. In some jurisdictions grey water reuse is forbidden or subject to complex sewage regulations which act as a deterrence to its adoption, but support is growing as experts continue to recognise that the wider environmental benefits outweigh the risks to health, which are insignificant if simple safeguards are followed.

Sustainable Urban Drainage

The conventional approach to dealing with rainwater in cities is to channel it into drains and watercourses in order to send it downstream as quickly as possible. This discharge is polluted and can often cause flooding downstream. Drains may be overwhelmed during storms and where foul water sewers are connected with surface drains (so-called combined sewers), and when surface water flooding occurs, this can lead to sewage leaving the sewers and threatening potable water supplies and aquatic ecosystems. Sustainable drainage systems (SuDS) have been developed in recent decades as a way of overcoming these problems.[14] The aim with SuDS is to reduce the volume and speed of surface water runoff, to improve water quality and to increase amenity. SuDS work initially by intercepting rainfall at source (where it lands) on green roofs or in rainwater harvesting systems (water butts or storage tanks). In most jurisdictions, rainwater that has been harvested can be used to flush toilets or for irrigation. Water that flows beyond green roofs or rainwater harvesting systems, may enter rills, rain gardens, swales and various ponds, to be detained, attenuated (slowed) or cleaned. Where soils and underlying geology is suitable, surface waters may be allowed to percolate into the ground, thereby recharging aquifers.

Water Sensitive Urban Design

A concept developed in Australia, Water Sensitive Urban Design (WSUD), goes beyond the aims of SuDS and recognises that surface drainage is an opportunity to bring ecosystem services to the city. There is also an intention to reduce potable water demand and therefore water abstraction, increase biodiversity, increase evapo-transpirative cooling and, where appropriate, store and clean grey water and storm water for reuse. WSUD considers the whole water cycle and not just urban surface water runoff. WSUD begins with the conservation of nature, where streams, rivers and wetlands are protected, restored and enhanced. Maintaining good water quality by cleaning water that drains from urban areas also protects the natural environment, not just streams and rivers but the estuaries and oceans that lie beyond. As with SuDS, the practitioners of WSUD seek to keep surface water within multi-functional landscapes, which can provide wildlife habitat and open space for people. Put simply, the idea is to mimic pre-development conditions, with similar runoff rates, water quality and biodiversity. Of course it is not possible to match pre-development conditions, but there is much to be gained by aiming high.[15,16]

Rain Gardens

In the USA, in cities, including Portland, Oregon, low impact development encourages a similar approach to WSUD, where people are encouraged to see surface water as more of an asset than a problem, feeding rain gardens and helping to prepare communities for the more extreme weather predicted to come with climate change (see figure 7.1).[17]

Rain gardens are shallow basins of permeable soil usually planted with perennial native plants. They are only one of many interventions associated with WSUD, including green roofs, water butts, permeable paving, swales and ponds; however, in the USA they have brought sustainable drainage away from the closed grey world of town planning and engineering and into the public consciousness. People are coming to understand that drainage can be beautiful, with attractive plants in low maintenance arrangements providing habitat for butterflies and other wildlife. In many cities in the USA, the authorities are now encouraging people to build rain gardens on their own properties, with plenty of detailed guidance available.[18] The simple but powerful idea of rain gardens is spreading rapidly.

The Streets are Changing

Much of our urban runoff comes from streets. Pollutants from vehicles, including oils, oil combustion products and heavy metals accumulate

Figure 7.1 Roadside rain garden in Portland, Oregon.

Figure 7.2 Before and after in a street in Portland, Oregon. Traffic calming combined with rain gardens.

on sealed surfaces and are washed into drains and ultimately into streams, following rainfall. Most streets have trees and some have grass verges or planters, but these plantings normally receive only the rainfall that falls upon them. Unless they are irrigated, street plantings may be more vulnerable to drought than plants not surrounded by sealed surfaces. Often planters are raised or protected by continuous raised kerbs, preventing runoff from pavements or streets from entering the soil. Practitioners of WSUD see conventional street planting beds as a wasted opportunity. Simple modifications to kerbs can allow surface water to flow into the soil, irrigating the vegetation and enabling soil microbes to remove pollutants before they reach drains or streams. As with rain gardens, soils need to be modified to make them free-draining, and planting has to be matched to the hydrological conditions, which will include occasional inundation. Depending on the local topography and geology, street planting pits and trenches can be interconnected, soak away to recharge groundwater or overflow to conventional drains. Infiltration beds planted with trees and shrubs have also been successfully integrated into traffic calming schemes, where islands are created on areas of former asphalt.

Ponds

Sustainable drainage schemes are characterised by engineers as having a series of stages beginning with source control (for example green roofs or rainwater harvesting tanks), conveyance and infiltration/filtration (for example swales) and finally attenuation and discharge of storm water, which often involves the use of ponds. There is a common misconception

Figure 7.3 Royal Park, Melbourne, where surface water from a wide area is collected and stored in lakes for irrigation.

that sustainable drainage must involve ponds and when insufficient space for a pond is available in an inner city area it is sometimes assumed that sustainable drainage may not be possible; however, combinations of rainwater harvesting, green roofs, rain gardens and other features may be enough to return runoff rates to pre-development levels. Ponds, however, are desirable: they can constitute valuable habitats in their own right and can act as reservoirs, making irrigation of vegetation during drought possible. Ponds can also include substantial areas of marginal aquatic vegetation, which is an effective way of removing water-borne pollution and sediments. A useful way of using ponds as part of a water-sensitive approach to urban design is to locate ponds in local parks, where they can become more than ornamental features. Figure 7.3 shows a lake in Royal Park, Melbourne, which receives runoff from an urban catchment. Water is occasionally used for irrigation of the park. Another approach is to create dry, usually grassland, basins in open spaces, which can be allowed to flood temporarily following severe rainstorms.

Potsdamer Platz

It was once one of the busiest places in Europe, but was flattened during World War II and cut through by the Berlin Wall during the Cold War. Then after reunification Potsdamer Platz was redeveloped with a large number of commercial buildings. The Daimler-Chrysler scheme, part of the Potsdamer Platz redevelopment, is unremarkable to look at from the street, but what is interesting in terms of water is that this is a zero discharge site, with no surface water runoff to drains except in the case of the most exceptional storms. Zero discharge, which is commonly encountered in Germany, is achieved in this case through a combination of high-level extensive green roofs, lower level roof gardens and then a well-vegetated lake above a car park. Much of the rain that falls on the green roofs – typically more than 50% – evaporates. The rest enters the lake where it is stored and used to flush toilets and for irrigation. This approach means that the complex uses less potable water, is cooler in hot weather and has attractive green space which provides wildlife habitat at all levels.[19]

River Restoration

Most of our urban rivers and streams have been simplified and ecologically degraded. Larger watercourses lose their natural banks and bankside vegetation, which are replaced with vertical walls. They also lose their connection with their floodplains because embankments are established. Smaller watercourses are often culverted, that is, lined with concrete or put into underground pipes. Such practices have led to a marked

Figure 7.4 River restoration, Sutcliffe Park, Lewisham, south-east London. Shortly after opening (left) and a few years later (right).

deterioration in water quality, catastrophic loss of habitat for fish and other wildlife and severance of ecological corridors as well as the loss of amenity. Recognising these problems, as the 20th century drew to a close, a few pioneers began to successfully argue for, and demonstrate the feasibility of, the restoration of rivers. Soft vegetated banks can replace steel and concrete, meanders can be put back and natural river-bed features reinstated. Even streams that had disappeared under-ground decades ago have been 'daylighted' – brought back to the surface. An example of a stream daylighting project is the Saw Mill River in Yonkers, New York. Put into a pipe by the Army Corp of Engineers in the 1920s, work began in 2010 to make the stream visible again to the public, who will be able to enjoy the view and will be better able to appreciate the importance of healthy streams. Special attention is being paid to the restoration of habitat for fish, notably the American eel.[20] In south-east London, the River Quaggy once flowed through a culvert in Sutcliffe Park. A restoration project completed in 2003 was able to reduce flood risk whilst improving the park. A new low-flow meander was created and part of the park lowered to provide a flood storage area with wetlands and boardwalks (see figure 7.4). The park has become more popular and the success of this project is encouraging others to look for similar opportunities within the catchment and elsewhere in London.[21,22]

The Cheonggyecheon River

Beginning in 1958 the Cheonggyecheon River in Seoul, South Korea was gradually buried in an underground culvert and by 1976 covered with a

Figure 7.5 'Daylighted' sections of the Cheongyecheon River, Seoul, South Korea.

double-decker multi-lane highway. Seoul suffers from a lack of green space and when Lee Myung-bak (now President of South Korea) stood for Mayor in 2002 he promised to daylight the Cheonggyecheon River in order to address this problem. Once elected, he pursued the project with determination, overcoming objections from local businesses and by people concerned with traffic congestion. Once opened in 2005, the project soon won favour (see figure 7.5). What had been created was a 5.8 kilometre long linear park, with clean flowing water and an abundance of wildlife.[23] People flock to the park, enticed by the relative quiet and cooler temperatures in the height of summer. Air quality has improved as traffic has declined, but the most remarkable change brought about by the project has been the catalyst for the regeneration of the whole downtown area, with Cheonggyecheon uniting people living north and south. The park has become new cultural centre. There are criticisms. The project is not a true river restoration and consists of an artificial watercourse sitting above a pipe. Campaigners have suggested that the $281 million budget would have been better spent on ecological restoration throughout the whole catchment. That may be true, but the project is a demonstration of how green infrastructure can revitalise a city and be an inspiration for others.

Singapore

Singapore is an equatorial island city-state of 5 million people. It can only collect 20% of its water supply from its own internal catchments

Figure 7.6 River restoration in Bisham Park, Singapore.

and relies on neighbouring Malaysia for much of its water. In 2001, an integrated approach to water management was adopted when the Public Utilities Board was given responsibility for both water supply and sanitation. Singapore is now committed to a long-term objective of providing all of its own water, from rainwater collection and storage, reclamation (cleaning wastewater or grey water) and desalination by 2061, when the current water supply agreement with Malaysia expires. This commitment has focused minds and given rise to a number of very interesting projects, including a campaign to reduce water consumption but also programmes to encourage people to respect and enjoy spending time near water bodies, most of which are reservoirs. Of special note is the Kallang River – Bishan Park river restoration project (see figure 7.6), one of several throughout the island.[24] This project, which is the result of collaboration between the Public Utilities Board and the National Parks Board, involves the removal of concrete and the restoration of a meandering channel flanked by marginal aquatic vegetation. The project will create wildlife habitat, help to clean water destined for a reservoir and will provide playgrounds for children, who are being encouraged to spend more time exercising in the outdoors. River restoration in tropical locations is particularly challenging because of heavy and frequent rainfall and the authorities have experimented with a number of bioengineering techniques in order to ensure that bank stability is not comprised by the establishment of vegetation and riparian habitat features.

Water and Urban Heat Islands

The rapid drying of the exposed hard and dense surfaces in the urban environment and the subsequent severe reduction in evaporation that occurs with conventional urban development is the main cause of the urban heat island effect. The relationship between temperature and land use is made very clear with city heat maps, where green space is several degrees cooler than adjacent built-up districts. Good examples are Richmond Park and Hampstead Heath in London, which show up as cool islands on the London heat map.[25] It is therefore very important that soil, soil water, water and vegetation are conserved and restored to the urban environment, not only to reduce the risk of flooding and to improve the quality of water in watercourses but also to maintain evaporative cooling. This changes our view of surface water and evaporation from being a nuisance and loss to being an enhancement, something that is now being recognised.

Towards the Water Sensitive City

We know that there is a need for change in the way that water flows through the city. Too much potable water is abstracted from watercourses and aquifers to be piped, pumped and consumed. Per capita consumption needs to be reduced. Soil has been sealed, making cities hot and dry. That must be reversed. Rivers have been straightened and deepened in the misguided belief that that will make us safer. That also must be reversed, wherever possible. Downstream water bodies, estuaries and even the oceans have been degraded by urban runoff and wastewater. A clean-up is long overdue. As pioneers have demonstrated, changing the way that cities deal with water will change their appearance. Cities can support more vegetation and city watercourses can be clean places full of wildlife, thereby becoming more of a community and economic asset. Increasing evapo-transpiration helps to keep cities cool, and increasing the amount of exposed soil reduces rainwater runoff, so we can see that the water-sensitive city of the future will be more resilient to the floods and droughts that are predicted to increase with climate change. The next chapter develops the theme of ecological restoration and considers how people are bringing nature into the city.

8. City-wide Greening

A bioregion refers to both the geographical terrain and a terrain of consciousness – to a place and the ideas that have developed about how to live in that place

– Peter Berg

Bioregions

City greening needs to go beyond the city boundary. Take, for example, the bioregion concept, which was devised by Peter Berg and Ray Dasmann in the 1970s.[1] Bioregions are usually defined as watersheds, within which there are similar terrains, climates, soils, biomes and landscape character. The term bioregionalism has come to encapsulate a philosophy where people adopt a sustainable lifestyle through the consumption of locally produced food and materials. It has even been suggested that bioregionalism spawned much of the green movement in North America.[2] Cities exist within a bioregional hinterland, and although modern commerce allows cities to operate in a global marketplace, it makes sense for communities to source goods and services from within the bioregion in order to reduce the production of greenhouse gases produced during transportation. It has also been observed that food produced locally is fresh and tends to have a better taste. Of course, national, provincial and municipal boundaries rarely coincide with watershed boundaries, especially in the lowlands,

Ecosystem Services Come to Town: Greening Cities by Working with Nature,
First Edition. Gary Grant.

which means that cooperation between authorities is essential if the bioregional approach is to work.

Catchment Management for Clean Water

Most of the water consumed by the majority of cities comes from within the bioregion, and wise management of the catchment (known as the watershed in the US) reduces the investment required in energy-hungry, conventional, grey infrastructure. An example of this approach is the way that watersheds are protected in New York State (namely the Catskill, Delaware and Crotons watersheds), where drinking water is collected and stored in order to supply New York City (see figure 8.1).[3] It has been estimated that the protection of these watersheds will cost the city around $1.5 billion, but this should be compared with an estimated $6–8 billion which would be required for additional water filtration plants if

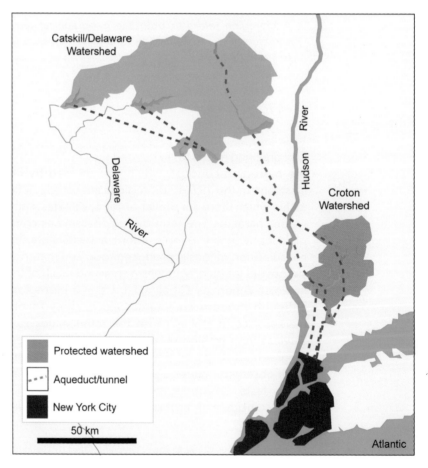

Figure 8.1 The New York City water supply system relies on watershed protection.

those watersheds were ever to be degraded or developed. An arrangement to protect these watersheds was agreed in 1997 and involved a partnership agreement between the Environmental Protection Agency, State of New York, New York City, communities located throughout the watershed and non-governmental organisations. Understandably, some people living and working within the rural catchment were concerned about possible limitations on their activities and the catchment management agreement followed years of discussions. Once an agreement had been reached, it allowed New York City to acquire land in the watershed and the partners to issue various watershed management regulations and initiate water quality protection programmes.

Catchment Management for Ecosystem Services

Protected catchments are not just places where rain falls before being filtered and stored; they are landscapes where a range of other ecosystem goods and services are provided. City people can reach these places to relax, exercise and enjoy the fresh air. Such places are usually within easy travelling distance of the conurbations that they serve, and in some places they are within walking distance. A good example of this is the country parks of Hong Kong, originally established as water catchment areas, that cover about 40% of uplands of the territory.[4] The protection of a reliable supply of drinking water may have been the primary focus of the authorities in New York, but catchment management for the maintenance of salmon fisheries has been an important motive for the authorities in Oregon. The capture and canning of salmon really took off in the 1870s and soon became one of the main exports of the state. A serious decline in the salmon fishery was already evident by the beginning of the 20th century, probably caused by large-scale logging (which led to siltation of rivers), water pollution, water abstraction (for irrigation of crops) and overfishing. As the 20th century progressed, a series of hydroelectric dams were constructed along the Columbia River and its tributaries, which blocked access to thousands of kilometres of streams, which had been the spawning grounds for salmon. By the 1970s, as conservation regulations were being passed, some salmon species were becoming endangered. By the 1990s Federal regulations were beginning to address water quality problems being caused by discharges from municipal storm sewers and so storm water management plans were developed in the cities. Typical initiatives included downpipe disconnection programmes (whereby rainwater from roofs was redirected to rain gardens). In subsequent years, efforts across the urban catchment, especially in Portland, led to better coordination of efforts between departments (in 2001 the City of Portland – the largest city in the state – established a Sustainable Infrastructure Committee)[5] and incentives

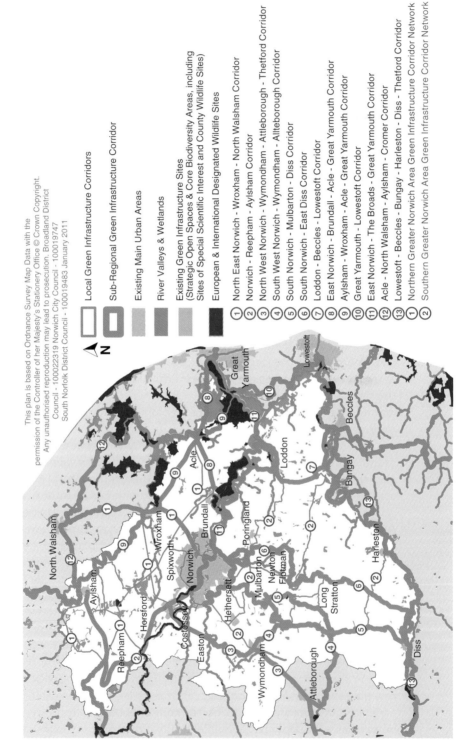

This plan is based on Ordnance Survey Map Data with the
permission of the Controller of her Majesty's Stationery Office © Crown Copyright.
Any unauthorised reproduction may lead to prosecution. Broadland District
Council - 100022319 Norwich City Council - 100019747
South Norfolk District Council - 100019483 January 2011

N

Local Green Infrastructure Corridors

Sub-Regional Green Infrastructure Corridor

Existing Main Urban Areas

River Valleys & Wetlands

Existing Green Infrastructure Sites
(Strategic Open Spaces & Core Biodiversity Areas, including
Sites of Special Scientific Interest and County Wildlife Sites)

European & International Designated Wildlife Sites

1 North East Norwich - Wroxham - North Walsham Corridor
2 Norwich - Reepham - Aylsham Corridor
3 North West Norwich - Wymondham - Attleborough - Thetford Corridor
4 South West Norwich - Wymondham - Allteborough Corridor
5 South Norwich - Mulbarton - Diss Corridor
6 South Norwich - East Diss Corridor
7 Loddon - Beccles - Lowestoft Corridor
8 East Norwich - Brundall - Acle - Great Yarmouth Corridor
9 Aylsham - Wroxham - Acle - Great Yarmouth Corridor
10 Great Yarmouth - Lowestoft Corridor
11 East Norwich - The Broads - Great Yarmouth Corridor
12 Acle - North Walsham - Aylsham - Cromer Corridor
13 Lowestoft - Beccles - Bungay - Harleston - Diss - Thetford Corridor
1 Northern Greater Norwich Area Green Infrastructure Corridor Network
2 Southern Greater Norwich Area Green Infrastructure Corridor Network

Figure 8.2 The Greater Norwich Green Infrastructure Plan.

schemes were established to encourage the creation of rain gardens and other sustainable drainage features like green roofs (known locally as eco-roofs).

Regional Green Infrastructure Plans

In the UK, regional (or sub-regional) green infrastructure plans have been prepared by partnerships of local authorities. This has usually occurred where rapid population growth is anticipated. An example is the Greater Norwich area in the East of England (see figure 8.2), where a consortium of rural and city authorities, assisted by planners and ecologists in Norfolk County Council and the Norfolk Wildlife Trust, is wrestling with the problem of providing ecosystem services to an additional 90,000 people by 2026.[6,7] The sub-region's Green Infrastructure Strategy shows how green space will link the towns and cities together with the wider countryside, providing cycling and walking routes, and prioritising areas where wildlife habitat can be restored. There is a strong emphasis on improving the management of flood risk and many of the proposed green infrastructure corridors follow river valleys.

Biomass and the Bioregion

Targets to reduce the production of greenhouse gases and to reduce reliance on fossil fuels mean that biomass production to feed a new wave of efficient district level electricity generation and combined heat and power plants is being widely promoted. Since the early 1990s, Sweden has pioneered the cultivation of short-rotation coppice as an energy crop. There are now also many substantial short-rotation coppice projects in France, Germany and the UK.[8] Willows (Salix species) grow back from the rootstock after being cut. Once established, a crop can be taken from willow every three years. These fast-growing trees can flourish on a variety of soils and can also be used to clean wastewater discharged from sewage treatment plants. Large plantations are required to provide the huge volumes of material needed to feed power plants, and fuel should ideally be within easy reach, so the green belts and rural hinterlands of city-regions may be suited to the production of this kind of energy crop. Other locations that are being considered for energy crops are derelict sites in former industrial areas, where there may also be the possibility of removing contamination by using vegetation – so called phytoremediation.[9] An example of a region with plenty of derelict sites, which could be used to grow energy crops, is the Black Country, in the historic industrial area in the West Midlands of England (see figure 8.3). This region, which has a population of approximately 1 million, is also surrounded by a green

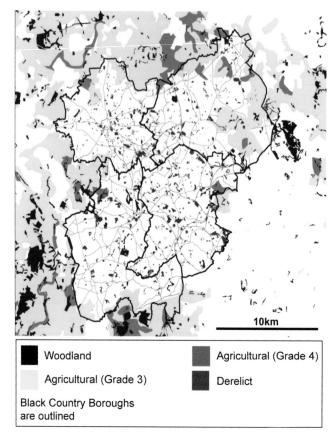

Figure 8.3 Potential for biomass crop cultivation in and around the Black Country (English West Midlands).

belt and open countryside where further biomass crops including willows and other trees could be grown.

Regional Ecological Networks

The Netherlands has a National Spatial Strategy, which guides patterns of land use throughout the country, which is explained in detail through various plans and documents, including for example the National Ecological Network. These high level strategies have been translated into an action plan, known as 'Beautiful Netherlands'. Provinces and cities have a close relationship with the national authorities and prepare enforceable regional plans. For example, the Province of Noord-Brabant, which includes the towns of Den Bosch and Eindhoven, like other provinces, has prepared a detailed ecological network plan.[10] This regional plan is compatible with and is a subset of, the overarching National Ecological Network, which is expected to be in place on the ground by 2018.[11] In order to cope with the challenges of making the man-made rural and urban landscape permeable to wildlife, the Dutch have developed the concept of green-blue veining, where usually linear and sometimes relatively narrow elements are used to make connections. These small-scale features include hedges, streams, ditches, banks and tree lines, so they can be no more than a few metres in width in some cases. Local authorities, however, are also alert to the benefits of establishing larger, robust connectors, usually new multi-functional parks but sometimes areas where the emphasis is primarily on restoring wildlife habitats or bridging over features such as railways or major roads that prevent wildlife crossing the landscape. The national framework is an important tool in identifying priority locations for such interventions (like green bridges), which tend to be very expensive and therefore need detailed justification.

Community Forests

Another approach to greening the city-region is to establish partner-ships or non-governmental organisations to plant forests on farmland or former quarries or industrial sites. Initially these projects, which in the UK date from the 1980s, were opportunistic in terms of site selection, but are increasingly being coordinated with proposed landscape-scale ecological networks. The National Forest in the English Midlands is one such project. Occupying much of the countryside between Leicester and Burton-on-Trent, it covers more than $500\,km^2$ where 7.8 million trees have been planted in hundreds of locations and woodland cover has increased from 6% to 18%. These forest projects have an impres-sive record of community engagement and fundraising. Originally conceived as regeneration projects in economically depressed areas, these new forests are now also being promoted as nature conservation schemes and climate change mitigation and adaptation measures.[12]

Green Belts

Fear of urban sprawl in the 1930s promoted the Campaign for the Protection for Rural England (CPRE) to call for green belts or areas of rural land to be permanently protected in order to prevent adjacent conurbations coalescing. Green belts were established around most of the major cities, including London, and now England has 14 green belt areas covering 13% of the land surface.[13] The idea was exported to many countries including Australia, Canada (notably Ottawa)[14] and certain states in America, including Oregon and Tennessee (where they are known as Urban Growth Boundaries). The concept has suc-ceeded in terms of preventing some of the excesses of urban sprawl

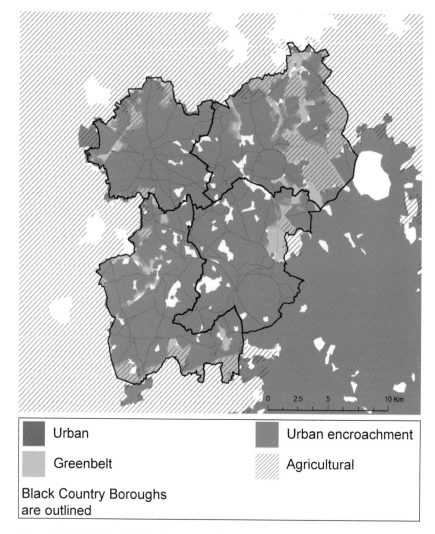

Figure 8.4 The West Midlands green belt.

seen for example in some US cities, and the concept is very popular with the public but there is a common misconception that green belt land has high landscape or ecological quality, which is rarely the case. Green belt has sometimes become the favoured alignment for major new transportation routes and has been cited as the cause of land-hungry suburban developments being developed even further away from the urban centre, that is, beyond the green belt. Existing green belts, however, are now being seen as important connectors between regional ecological and green infrastructure networks and the finer intra-urban green space networks and there is usually the potential for large-scale ecological restoration or the creation of new 'countryside parks' that can provide a rural experience relatively close to home for city dwellers, taking the pressure off of some of the more sensitive natural areas that may be further afield. Where regional biomass for energy schemes are being considered, there is also the possibility of green belt being used to provide the fuel. Green belts will still feature in future cities, but are likely to become more accessible and likely to fulfil a number of roles, acting as the coupling between the city green space network and the wider countryside. It is also likely that as interest in local food continues to build, market gardens (vegetable farms) will make a return to green belts.

Green Grids

In an echo of Abercrombie's plans for chains of open space in London, hatched during World War II, the Mayor of London's office is now promoting the All London Green Grid (see figure 8.5). The initiative is seen as breathing new life into green space policy in order to provide a new generation of parks that will help Londoners to adapt to climate change and population growth. The authorities in London have also recognised a need for better coordination so that individual parcels of green space, whether parks, river corridors, cemeteries or nature reserves, are physically linked together and made more accessible. The Green Grid began in east London (the East London Green Grid), where more than 300 green infrastructure projects have been identified.[15] Access to the Grid and the concept of the whole enterprise is being highlighted through a series of walking routes. The East London Green Grid is strongly associated with river valleys and builds on work that has been undertaken in the past, notably the Lee Valley Regional Park, which has in effect been extended into the built-up part of London's East End through the creation of the new Queen Elizabeth Olympic Park (QEOP) and the Fatwalk, which will link the QEOP with the River Thames.[16]

Transport

Transportation corridors, in the form of major roads and railways, often include substantial verges, embankments and cuttings, which can act as ecological corridors. Vegetation along these corridors is often lightly managed and can become species-rich and ecologically valuable. Railway lines have been designated as local wildlife sites and can constitute a significant proportion of ecologically important land in inner city sites.[17] Transportation corridors may allow some fauna, such as reptiles and amphibians for example, to move from open countryside into city centres but these sites are also vulnerable to colonisation by invasive non-native plants (like *Buddliea davidii* in London

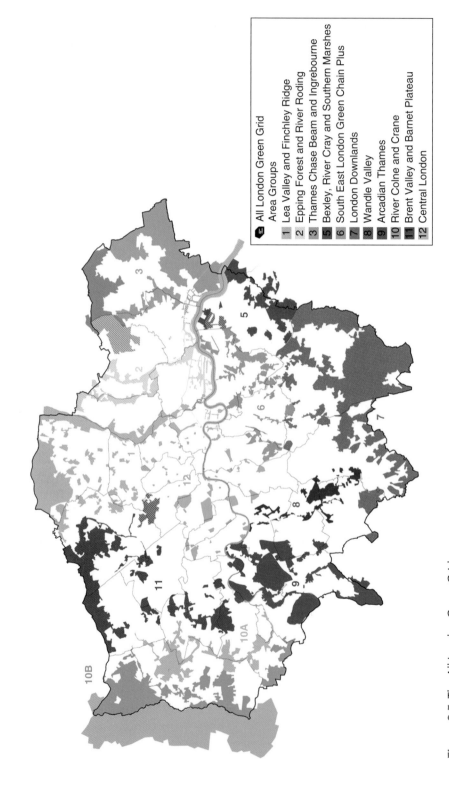

Figure 8.5 The All London Green Grid.

All London Green Grid
Area Groups
1 Lea Valley and Finchley Ridge
2 Epping Forest and River Roding
3 Thames Chase Beam and Ingrebourne
5 Bexley, River Cray and Southern Marshes
6 South East London Green Chain Plus
7 London Downlands
8 Wandle Valley
9 Arcadian Thames
10 River Colne and Crane
11 Brent Valley and Barnet Plateau
12 Central London

for example). Railways and roads, especially, tend to fragment higher quality habitats and act as a barrier to the movement of some species of wildlife as well as pedestrians. City planning authorities are now becoming more aware of these problems and are identifying where crossing points (for both wildlife and people) would be most effective. There are also attempts to coordinate the planning of transportation routes and green infrastructure networks, for example in Thomas Jefferson Planning District around Charlottesville, Virginia.[18] The integrated approach to planning adopted around Charlottesville, however, is still uncommon, and in most urban jurisdictions in the world there is still an emphasis on, at best, mitigating impacts of new transportation projects rather than using these as an opportunity to restore ecosystems. Perhaps the easiest and most promising combination of green infrastructure and transport planning, however, is where strategic cycling and walking routes are created, facilitating and the physical linkage of habitats and green space.

Urban Heat Islands

The authorities in major metropolitan areas are increasingly aware of urban heat islands, where built-up inner city districts are appreciably hotter than surrounding areas. The mapping of urban heat islands has influenced the way some cities are preparing green infrastructure strategies. For example, the City of Manchester in north-west England has identified a strategic inner city axis, the Oxford Road corridor, where it is hoped that by implementing a series of green infrastructure projects, including tree planting and the retrofitting of green roofs, the urban heat island can be reduced. In many conurbations, analysis of the spatial arrangement of other factors including social deprivation, populations with health problems, air quality and vulnerability to flash flooding shows that there is often an overlap between these problems and urban heat islands, reinforcing the call for green infrastructure interventions (see figure 8.6).

Blue Networks

Rivers and coastal waters are major features in many cities and city-regions. In the past, such areas were often relegated to little more than sewers or potential sources of new (reclaimed) land, but planners are now recognising the importance of these areas. The term 'blue infrastructure' is often used to describe rivers and coastal waters. These areas provide relief from the city. They are cooler in summer and are usually important habitats, for example providing nurseries for fish, and important areas for wintering, breeding and migratory birds. An

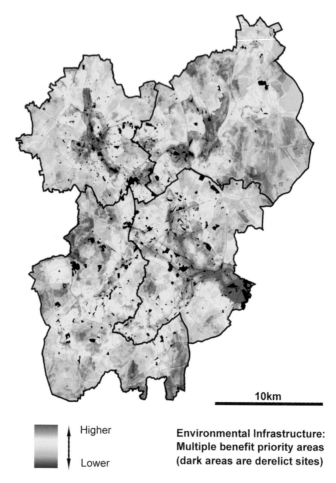

Higher

Lower

Environmental Infrastructure:
Multiple benefit priority areas
(dark areas are derelict sites)

Figure 8.6 An analysis of where green infrastructure interventions will bring multiple benefits in the English Black Country, reflecting the overlap between urban heat islands and other urban problems.

aspect of great significance is that blue infrastructure is often the only truly city-wide or regional natural feature, and riverside sites are often the only viable city-wide green infrastructure networks. Another issue is that land that is adjacent to watercourses is often prone to flooding. Fluvial flooding may be infrequent, but when it occurs in urban areas, it can be extremely costly. Sometimes, floodplains that had remained undeveloped for centuries have been built over, as the pace of urban development accelerated after World War II. Many authorities now recognise that it may be wise to protect floodplains from development, or even restore green space to previously developed floodplains in order to extend blue and green infrastructure networks. This approach is likely to gain momentum as climate change makes flooding more likely and the role of blue infrastructure becomes more important in reducing urban heat islands and providing space for recreation, wildlife habitat and food growing. Floodplain restoration is particularly important for ecological restoration because the wetlands that occupy transitional positions between aquatic and terrestrial habitats have largely disappeared, especially in urban situations. As floods occur, local authorities often reconsider their approach. An example is the London Borough of Sutton, where severe floods in 2007 are cited as a factor in the development of new policies to guide development within the river valley.[19]

Masterplanning

Where large-scale urban planning does occur, for example where former industrial sites are redeveloped for residential use, or where urban extensions are developed, the conventional planning approach is for grids of streets to be laid out and the plots 'populated' with buildings or open space according to standards and market demand. This approach creates serious obstacles for water, wildlife and pedestrians. A preferred approach is for any existing habitat to be retained and to use restored watercourses and associated greenspace to form the skeleton of the masterplan. Surface water drainage networks, main footpaths and cycleways can then be planned to ensure walkability and accessibility to greenspace. Even if conventional grid street patterns are subsequently adopted, this ecologically sensitive approach results in a markedly different pattern of development. An example is the influential mixed-use development of the disused Stapleton Airport, Denver, where a stream which had been buried under the airport runway, was brought to the surface (daylighted) and restored to form the open space spine of the new community of 30,000 people (see figure 8.7).[20] The new greenspace network interconnects with existing open spaces and is within easy reach of the various new neighbourhoods. There is plenty of wildlife habitat and many combinations of useful and interesting routes for both walkers and cyclists. The whole scheme was developed in the 1990s according to a 'Green Book' vision agreed by the various partners and stakeholders after two years of research and widespread community consultation. It may not be perfect, but it demonstrates how green infrastructure planning and a concern for better management of surface waters is beginning to influence the masterplanning process and to stretch and bend conventional rectilinear grids, at least here and there.

Regional Plans, Local Implementation

Although city-regions always sit within a watershed (or watersheds) and almost always consist of landscapes of habitat fragments separated by roads and urban development – where strategic planning is

Figure 8.7 Masterplan for mixed use development at the former Stapleton Airport site, Denver.

Figure 8.8 Restored river in new green space, Stapleton, Denver.

important – implementation of projects is usually undertaken at a local level by a number of different actors. This illustrates the importance of local projects being implemented by people who are fully aware of high-level planning, in terms of watershed management, ecological network planning or site masterplanning. The valuable work that has been done in regional ecological planning does not always translate into the most appropriate projects at a local level, perhaps because people are not aware of strategic planning, or, when they are, because other priorities take precedence. Another difficulty is that the idea of a network implies prioritisation, and projects which fall outside of the boundaries of a network may not receive all the attention to ecological or hydrological matters that they should. Networks may help us to prioritise limited resources, but the principles of ecological restoration and water sensitivity should and can be pursued anywhere. The next chapter looks in more detail at how such local neighbourhood and building-level greening works.

9. Greening Neighbourhoods and Buildings

Think Globally, Act Locally

– Rene Dubos

Sense of Neighbourhood

Experts find it difficult to agree on a definition of a neighbourhood, but most people intuitively sense where their neighbourhood begins and ends, because it is an area centred on their home or place of work, where they meet and greet people they know on a regular basis. When people do not regularly meet and greet, a sense of neighbourhood fades. Within that neighbourhood there may be the public realm, including the local parks and streets as well as the buildings in which people live and work. The neighbourhood or precinct is the building block for the green city and this is where the greatest potential lies for local projects, initiated, supported and sustained by citizens. Buildings are often the main focus. Buildings are important and are considered later in this chapter, but a collection of buildings is not enough on its own to create a functioning or attractive neighbourhood. Small-scale neighbourhood projects are often overlooked by planning and design professionals, who tend to be assigned to (and are often entranced by) large-scale expensive schemes which feature on city-wide maps; however, thousands of small neighbourhood projects can coalesce and combine to transform districts and, ultimately, whole cities. This

Ecosystem Services Come to Town: Greening Cities by Working with Nature, First Edition. Gary Grant.

chapter considers small-scale projects at neighbourhood and building scale, which will ultimately constitute the transformational change which many of us now seek.

Living Streets

Clearly the kind of social network that depends on so-called *face time* will be disrupted if people are in their car and not on foot or on their bike. Donald Appleyard's pioneering study in the late1970s found that the residents of streets with light traffic had three more friends and twice as many acquaintances as similar people on otherwise similar streets with heavy traffic.[1] The perception of safety is also important, because children are less likely to be corralled indoors by nervous parents, and older people will feel the confidence to venture out, if motor vehicle traffic is limited and if there are parks, gardens and squares to relax in. In the 1970s, in the Netherlands, *Woonerfs* were first established. They are streets where pedestrians and cyclists have priority over motorists and speed limits are kept low. By the turn of the century there were more than 6000 such areas in the Netherlands and the idea had spread across much of Europe. Once it was appreciated that promoting eye contact between pedestrians and motorists is more effective than speed limit signs and regulations, the shared space concept, where all users have equal priority, became the new objective.[2] The living streets concept takes the idea a stage further, with pedestrians given priority over motor vehicles. Paving treatments, chicanes, the absence of kerbs and the provision of seating

Figure 9.1 Brighton New Road. Street improvements by Gehl Architects, where motorists and pedestrians share space on equal terms.

are used to create streets where motorists drive slowly and tentatively. Signs and barriers, which have been shown through research by Jan Gehl and others to have no influence on safety, are kept to a minimum, so that streets can be de-cluttered and made more inviting.[3] Although shared space or living streets projects are not primarily about greening, they do encourage a healthier lifestyle (by encouraging walking and cycling) and de-cluttering often does provide opportunities for planting trees or creating planters or rain gardens. With more people taking their time to enjoy the street, they are surely more likely to take an interest in the comfort and beauty provided by vegetation.

Standardising the Neighbourhood

In the developed world, the participation of citizens in the greening of neighbourhoods has been relegated to an indirect role, whereby people are primarily consumers of local government services. In other words you can complain to an official or politician if something irks you, and if a defect is confirmed because of a lack of conformity with official standards or guidance, and if it is affordable, action will be taken. This illustrates the importance of standards, but greening falls behind with this approach because, until recently, standards have been compiled only for streets, paving, drains and lighting, with vegetation considered an optional extra. Municipalities are good at creating and maintaining urban forests of trees in parks and streets but they are not so adept at maintaining landscapes at ground level, where mechanisation has led to the preponderance of species-poor grasslands. Coupled with these difficulties is the widespread ignorance of the various benefits of vegetation and soil and a commonly held belief that the provision of planting is a matter of aesthetics alone. When local authorities have experienced difficulties with vegetated fragments of 'municipal landscapes', especially small sites and traffic islands, there has been a tendency to 'pave and forget' in the mistaken belief that asphalt deserts save time and money. This has not gone unnoticed by the guerrilla gardeners, now operating in 30 countries, who, frustrated by the sterility of their neighbourhoods, have taken action and planted their own vegetable or flowers gardens, often under the cover of darkness to avoid official interference.[4]

Design Your Own Park

Evolutionary biologist David Sloan Wilson studied the distribution of altruistic people in his home town of Binghampton, New York and noticed how clusters of these altruistic people occurred in various locations. Altruistic people (Wilson calls them 'prosocial') seem to attract and foster more altruistic people. He wondered if areas where there appeared to be little altruism could be turned around by initiating projects where people were given an opportunity to cooperate with their neighbours; this tends to bring people together and create a positive mood. In order to test his ideas on the ground, he has initiated five Design Your Own Park initiatives where people are creating parks of their own design on neglected ground.[5] The approach adopted in these projects is based on the ideas of Elinor Ostrom, who won the 2009 Nobel Prize for economic science.[6] Ostrom showed that people can cooperate to manage common resources to great effect if goals are defined, costs and benefits are shared equally, decision-making is through consensus, conflict resolution is fair, the group has autonomy and outside relationships are carefully structured. For example, Ostrom found that primitive communal farmer-managed irrigation systems are more efficient and effective than equivalent engineer-designed official government projects. The lesson is that people can make a good job of managing their own common ground if the right frameworks are in place. This can bring people together to do even more.

A Phoenix Rises

When citizens do participate in neighbourhood greening, the layout of space tends to be quite different from that typically found in conventional parks. Parks become more like gardens, are more intimate and have more character, with a high diversity and high density of planting. An example of this is the Phoenix Garden in London's West End, created by volunteers in 1984 on what had been a Second World War bombsite[7] (see figure 9.2). The involvement of a number of hands-on volunteers (including the author) in the establishment and maintenance meant that a large number of features are included in a small area, including many trees, shrubs, trellises, planting beds and seating, as well as a pond, compost bay and shelter. Installations from the early days that didn't work, like a sand pit, have been planted or adapted. As the garden has matured, there are minor difficulties created by perhaps a little too much shade as closely planted trees grow more quickly than people imagined they would, but the desire to increase biodiversity has given the garden a new impetus, with planting designed to attract wildlife, including bees and birds. The Phoenix Garden is little known outside of the immediate neighbourhood but is a great success with both local residents and workers, and is a venue for a number of regular community events. It achieves a great deal in a small space and has an intimate charm, which is absent from many municipal parks.

Figure 9.2 Phoenix Garden, established and maintained by the local community in London's West End.

Growing Their Own

The transfer of ownership and management from government to local communities, so-called 'asset transfer' tends to be focused on buildings, but is likely to be increasingly used to release green space in the future.[8] Current concern regarding the high cost of public services is encouraging officials and politicians to look closely at more wide-spread ownership and management of urban green space by local groups, not only for the provision of conventional parks but also to cater for the renewed interest in urban vegetable growing (known as allotments in the UK). In England and Wales, the Small Holdings and Allotments Act of 1908 obliged local authorities to provide vegetable plots to citizens at an affordable rent. A post-war decline in enthusiasm for this kind of gardening eventually led to sell-offs and redevelopment of some underused plots, but the decline has now been reversed, with shrill demands for new plots to be created. Now, organisations like the heritage charity, the National Trust, and local associations are helping to address the demand by providing new sites.[9] Within Europe there are allotment gardening federations in Austria, Belgium, Denmark, Finland, France, Germany, Luxembourg, the Netherlands, Norway, Poland, Slovakia, Sweden, Switzerland and the UK representing some 3 million people. In the USA, also, there are indications that local cooperation to encourage and foster food gardening is on the rise.[10]

Learning from Squatter Settlements

A number of researchers have looked carefully at the self-organised social and spatial arrangements of spontaneous informal (squatter) settlements and, contrary to conventional belief, have found a number of interesting and positive aspects. Neha Goel, who has studied the Khichripur slums of Delhi, India, sees squatter settlements as a self-organising process driven by family, clan and taboo, rather than simply a chaotic collection of buildings.[11] Although squatter settlements are characterised by poverty and inadequate infrastructure, they are remarkably efficient, flexible and resilient and provide people with attractive dwellings and workplaces with an excellent family and cultural life. People are often happier in squatter settlements than the planned and designed housing 'projects' into which they are moved by city authorities as slums are cleared. Architects and town planners are becoming interested in learning from the village-like urban vernacular, with its curved river-like pattern of car-free streets and hierarchies of public spaces (*chowk* in Hindi and Urdu), which form at junctions and often feature shade trees and water tanks (see figure 9.3). Private activities often spill over into, and animate, public spaces. Dwellings have a number of characteristics that provide adaptation to climate, including shared and thick external walls which increase shade and provide thermal mass and shaded courtyards to promote convective cooling. Rooms are multi-functional, carefully decorated and managed, and their use changes throughout the day. Owner-occupants are intimately involved in the building process – everyone knows what and how to build. The building techniques used suit everyone. Building forms are conservative and devoid of pretentious architectural styling, but there is a high level of flexibility of size, layout and decoration to suit individual families. The aim for those involved in urban renewal must surely be to take the attractive scale, organic form, flexibility, levels of participation and popularity of informal settlements and add to this the expensive – and by its nature centrally organised – infrastructure required to ensure health. There is also much to learn from the way that ordinary citizens are able to create such interesting places. Although it seems improbable that governments will ever relax their

Figure 9.3 Trees provide welcome shade in the Khichripur slum, Delhi.

control enough to allow people to self-build whole districts, modern easy-to-use design software has the potential to allow citizens to design and test virtual informal settlements. Such citizen-based virtual schemes could be translated into conventional drawings and documents by design professionals.

Rain Gardens

Community participation is definitely a resurgent force, but even where management remains with local government (as it will for most of the public realm) policy demands for the restoration of biodiversity and better storm water management are changing the way that neighbourhood green spaces work. Although watershed or catchment management provides an overarching framework for the planning of sustainable drainage, individual projects are often opportunistic and initiated at the neighbourhood level. A good example of this phenomenon is that of the rain gardens that are springing up in neighbourhoods throughout the USA. Authorities are devising clear policies, and knowledgeable and enthusiastic officers are providing excellent support in the form of technical advice; however, the invention and persistence of people is turning once overlooked and underused places into attractive and low-maintenance green spaces that are also a fully functioning parts of the drainage system. An excellent example

117

of partnership between the authorities responsible for catchment management and local involvement with neighbourhood greening is the Liberty Lands Park in Philadelphia, established as a community park in the 1990s. This 8000 m² park was renovated in 2009 in order to capture and store storm water from adjacent roads.[12] Water is cleansed by a series of rain gardens before it is stored in cisterns. It can then be used for irrigation if required. Another fascinating and inspiring way that neighbourhood greening is flourishing in Portland, Oregon, is where streets are being modified to include rain gardens. Conventional traffic engineering often involves verges and islands comprised of hard materials, but in Portland, where slope and topography permits, and often in places identified by local residents, kerbs are cut through to allow surface water to feed shallow basins filled with permeable soil and planted with a range of plants to suit the various conditions. (The rain gardens do flood after heavy rain but this is temporary and there are areas around the margins that remain fairly dry.) This diversity of topography, hydrology and predominantly native planting promotes biodiversity, and any trees planted nearby thrive because of the increase in soil moisture.

They Paved Paradise

Roads lead to parking lots, big and small. It has been estimated that parking lots make up 10% of the land surface of American cities so the problem is a significant one. Parking lots are some of the most barren places, quickly shedding rainfall, making a major contribution to urban heat islands and releasing oils and other pollutants into drains. The City of Toronto, Canada, has identified this problem and in 2007 issued new guidance to assist designers, developers and reviewers of schemes to widen their objectives.[13] This guidance makes it clear that the city will expect better consideration of the needs of pedestrians and cyclists in the future, and that existing trees and soils should be retained wherever possible. Porous paving will be used where feasible, and new landscape beds and lines of shade trees will be consolidated into adequately sized features. Importantly, the guidance indicates that rainwater and snowmelt should be directed into swales, which allow infiltration, evapo-transpiration and water reuse to take place. Similar guidance has been issued by many other North American and Australian cities, and many similar features are required by statute in Germany, Austria and Switzerland.

Clapton Park Estate

The Clapton Park Estate is a social housing scheme of about 1200 dwellings in Hackney, one of London's toughest inner city boroughs (see Figure 9.4). Since 2002, the management of the estate has been

Figure 9.4 Clapton Park Estate, Hackney, London.

undertaken by a small independent contracting firm led by John Little. He has ecological knowledge and engages with residents, both on a formal level through the residents' body and the managing agents, but also informally through open days and chats during routine working visits. This simple formula has led to a transformation of the grounds. Boundaries that were routinely treated with herbicide are now full of wild flowers and former species-poor lawns are now being used to grow vegetables. People are involved and the estate is a nicer place to live in, and the encouragement of biodiversity is not seen as a problem but a desirable goal.

People of the Trees

The planting of trees is probably the simplest and most popular way of greening streets and neighbourhoods. Trees were widely planted in cities during the 19th century for aesthetic purposes and have created a legacy of magnificent avenues, which in some cases are coming to the end of their life. This has prompted debate over whether or not like should be replaced with like or whether different, less problematic species should be used. For example, the great size of some trees as they reach maturity has caused concern in some cities, and trees have been blamed for exacerbating problems with older buildings with inadequate foundations, particularly on clay soils, which can shrink in drought and swell when re-wetted.[14] Pollution-tolerant species survived the soot and smog (for example, London plane and hybrid lime in London) and people came to realise that trees actually help to improve air quality by filtering particles and absorbing pollutants. More recently the role of trees in maintaining a pleasant microclimate, supporting wildlife, calming nerves and boosting property values has also become more widely appreciated. Information regarding the appropriate trees to plant is available from most local authorities, and urban tree planting is ably promoted by a number of non-governmental organisations such as Trees for Cities[15] and the Tree Council[16] in the UK, the National Tree Trust[17] in the USA, Planet Ark[18] in Australia and the International Tree Foundation[19] in Africa. China leads the world in tree planting initiatives, having held an annual tree planting day for more than 30 years, with more than 540 million people involved in tree planting each year.[20]

Tree Pits

Finding the space to plant trees in the inner city can be a real challenge, and there are whole districts where tree planting is not feasible. Trees can hinder access, block light and interfere with tall vehicles and lighting poles, signposts and overhead utilities, but it is the plethora of underground services that take up space under the street, which causes probably the most difficulty. The average modern city street has underground electricity, gas and telecommunication cables, potable water pipes and sewers, backfilled with aggregate, leaving little natural soil – inadequate and often unsuitable conditions for tree roots. Although the volume of a tree pit will vary according to species, climate and soil conditions, a typical tree requires $20\,m^3$ of soil at maturity.[21] At the point of planting, an excavation for a tree pit will normally be 900 mm by 900 mm wide and 750 mm deep (a volume of only $0.6\,m^3$), but of course the roots will spread beyond this as the tree grows. In the recent past, common practice has been to keep tree pits separated from drainage systems, but there is increasing interest in incorporating tree pits into sustainable drainage systems, to the benefit of the drainage system, but also the tree. In the past decade in Australia so-called bio-retention tree pits have been used to receive surface water runoff, with excess water overflowing into conventional

Figure 9.5 Tree pits designed to receive surface water runoff in Cordoba, Spain and dating from the 10th century.

drains.[22] The idea is not entirely new: for example, the patio of the oranges by the Grand Mosque in Cordoba, Spain was created in the 10th century (see Figure 9.5). Each tree pit receives surface runoff, and when they are full a channel in the surface paving sends water to the adjacent pit and so on.

Tree Trenches

Given the congestion and complexity of the underground environment of the modern street, the difficulties of finding space for trees and the urgent need to plant more trees in the face of climate change, efforts are underway to routinely provide purpose-made trenches for trees. 'Tree trenches' are a useful way of protecting underground services from roots but can also become a fully integrated component of the surface drainage system, being interconnected with

Figure 9.6 Infiltration trench with trees, Portland, Oregon.

underground water storage systems (storm cells) and with outlets that enter other downstream components or conventional drains. Examples of this approach can be seen in cities such as Nijmegen in the Netherlands and Philadelphia in the USA[23] (see figure 9.6).

No Space?

Sometimes, however, despite our best efforts, no room can be found for street trees, and a different approach is required. For example, in the City of London (the historic core of London) a combination of narrow, often medieval streets and modern underground services means that frequently the only opportunities for greening are on walls and roofs, and there is often an expectation that when a site is redeveloped, new space is provided at street level in the form of new piazzas or passageways under buildings. This approach leads to a blurring between the public and private realms, especially at street level, and an increasing reliance on the buildings as the platform for urban greening. With the heavy structures that predominate in city centres, there are many opportunities for retrofitting soil and vegetation, as is being demonstrated for instance at The Museum of London, in the Barbican, where the author's firm, the Green Roof Consultancy, is advising on the installation of roof gardens, extensive green roofs and living walls.[24]

Energy Efficient Buildings

For many, the greening of buildings and the built environment begins and ends with the reduction in energy consumption through intelligent design, high levels of insulation and the installation of efficient appliances. This approach is exemplified by the Passivhaus approach, conceived by Bo Adamson of Sweden and Wolfgang Feist of Germany in 1988. This meeting of minds led to the foundation of the Passivhaus-Institut in Darmstadt, Germany in 1996, and by 2003 the idea had gained a foothold in the USA. In Europe, the target of the Passivhaus approach is to reduce energy demand for space heating and cooling to less than 15 kWh/m²/year, which represents a reduction of more than 75% of the energy consumed by equivalent buildings meeting current US or UK standards.[25] Clearly this approach sets new standards that, once adopted, will result in huge reductions in energy use and associated CO_2 emissions. Of course, I commend energy conservation, but argue that greening should go far beyond this.

Water Efficiency

A similar approach, of increasing efficiency, can be applied to water consumption. The collection, cleaning and pumping of potable water is achieved through the consumption of surprisingly large quantities of electrical energy, which has a carbon footprint – water is said to have 'embodied carbon'. In developed countries this usually exceeds 1 tonne CO_2-equivalent per million litres (tCO₂e/Ml) and may even exceed 3tCO₂e/Ml if desalination is used. Water itself can be in short supply, and even where supplies appear to be secure, water that has been removed from rivers and aquifers may often cause the decline of ecosystems and the drying of the landscape. Water saving strategies include: metering (so as to be able to monitor consumption), prompt repair of leaks, having showers instead of baths and the use of water-efficient appliances.[26]

Autonomy

Beyond efficiency and conservation, however, there is the move towards more autonomy. A building can generate electricity through the use of photovoltaic (PV) cells or wind turbines. A typical domestic PV installation can generate around 40% of the electricity an average household uses on an annual basis.[27] Heat can be collected from the sun using solar hot water or from the ground using ground source heat pumps. Rainwater can be harvested from roofs and stored for reuse in toilet flushing or irrigation, and grey water (wastewater from washing)

Figure 9.7 Domestic rainwater harvesting system.

can also be treated and reused (although care is required in the use of grey water because it can contain pathogens).[28,29]

Building-integrated Vegetation

So the building is efficient in energy and water consumption. It may generate some or all of the energy it consumes. It may collect some of the water that it consumes. It will have the necessary systems in place to reduce and manage waste. Materials used in construction will have been chosen in order to minimise embodied carbon and to be locally appropriate. Now there is more that can be done. By bringing soil (growing media) and vegetation onto and around the building, biodiversity can be increased, but there will be additional benefits in terms of the thermal performance of the building, improvements to the local microclimate and reductions in surface water runoff.

A Coat for Buildings

Unlike most animals, which, if they are living in the open, have fur or hair to protect them, most buildings are 'naked', with building materials exposed to damaging ultraviolet light and extremes of temperature. By shielding these materials with soil and/or plants, their life can be extended by decades, and if the soil is deep enough, centuries. The

Figure 9.8 Wollishofen waterworks green roofs, near Zurich (established 1914).

asphalt-covered reinforced concrete roofs of the Moos Lake water filtration plant, constructed in Wollishofen, Zurich, Switzerland, in 1914, were exposed to the sun in their first summer of operation, causing the water within the buildings to overheat.[30] Warm water can promote the growth of pathogenic bacteria so action was required. The solution was to cover the roofs with layers of gravel and local soil (see figure 9.8) in order to shade the structure and promote evapo-transpirative cooling. In 2005, more than ninety years after construction, the waterproofing under the gravel and soil was inspected in a few locations and found to be in excellent condition. Exposed asphalt would not normally be expected to last more than 25 years before requiring repair and it can therefore be seen from the experience in Zurich that a green roof may more than quadruple the life of the waterproofing layer.

Value of Shade

Leaves may protect a building from the sun, intercepting up to 90% of the sunlight, using some of the energy in photosynthesis and reflecting the remainder. The reflectivity, or albedo, of leaves varies from a factor of 0.7 to 0.85, which is comparable to that of 'cool' roofs, which are painted white to reflect the sun's heat.[31] This protection can be in the form of an overshadowing tree, or scrambling, trailing or climbing plants closer to the structure. Vines have been shown to reduce the surface temperatures of walls by up to 20 °C on hot summer days and to reduce interior temperatures by more than 5 °C in similar

Figure 9.9 Climbing plants on the Stucki Shopping Centre, Basel, Switzerland.

conditions.[32,33] Deciduous plants may be particularly useful in temperate climates, shielding the building from the summer heat but allowing welcome winter sun to flood in. Evergreen climbing plants like common ivy can also have a beneficial effect in winter, reducing wind chill and creating a blanket of air on an outside wall. It is a widely held misconception that climbing plants, like common ivy, damage buildings. Research at Oxford University has shown that ivy provides a protective blanket around buildings, which extends the life of the building fabric.[34] If you are still not convinced and have concerns about plants clinging directly to buildings you can grow climbing plants on wires or frames, which can be removed for maintenance purposes (see figure 9.9).

Living Walls

Using climbing plants is an ancient and simple way of vegetating facades (or even roofs); however, during the last decade or so a number of new techniques have emerged. Inspired by the way tropical

Figure 9.10 Living wall at Quai Branly, by Patrick Blanc.

epiphytes thrive on tree trunks with no soil, the French botanist Patrick Blanc has pioneered the practical use of hydroponic living walls, where several species of plant of varying size and form grow from a thin layer of textiles attached to a backing board (see figure 9.10). His installations adorn a number of high-profile buildings throughout the world and have encouraged others to follow. Modular, scalable living wall systems have now appeared on the market and the competition is growing. Some systems are hydroponic (without soil) and rely on mineral wool, like the Biotecture system, whilst others consist of high-density polyethylene (HDPE) modules, which have cells that can be filled with growing medium and planted with a wide range of species. Other systems are based on plastic containers held in frames and fabric pockets. Living walls are irrigated, usually by means of pipes and emitters with varying levels of sophistication in terms of control. Some walls are periodically soaked, whilst others have a high level of automation, with sensors, which can trigger alarms or text messages if the wall dries because of component failure of the water being switched off. Living walls are reliant on irrigation and in most climates most species currently used will die if the water supply is interrupted. Wherever possible, captured rainwater or treated grey water should be used to irrigate living walls. Look at a broken downpipe on a shady wall and in most cities you will see wild ferns, mosses and other plants that grow from the brickwork and masonry. This suggests that it would be possible to load a modular wall with substrate and direct rainfall through it in order to create a low maintenance living wall that does not require irrigation. For the time being, however, living walls are planted with a range of popular horticultural plants. Invention and creativity is possible, but for success good horticultural knowledge is required, with planting carefully matched to aspect, local microclimate and the region in which the wall is created. Even with the benefit of irrigation, highly exposed walls that receive more sunshine are more difficult to cultivate than shady walls because of the high levels of evapo-transpiration, high exposure to sunlight and higher fluctuations in temperature that occur. The irrigation of living walls can be turned to good effect. Irrigation water can be passed through heat exchangers inside a building and the heat lost from the living wall. This has already been achieved in Hatton Wall in London, where heat from the computer servers in an office is being pumped to a Biotecture living wall in an outside courtyard. Even where heat exchangers are not used, however, living walls can create much cooler exterior microclimates and can shield what would otherwise be overheated high-density building materials from the sun's rays.

Cooling Effect of Green Roofs

Exposed building materials are usually dense and often dark, absorbing and storing the sun's radiation and reradiating some of this energy at night (the primary cause of the urban heat island effect). Where soil (or artificial growing medium, also known as substrate) occurs, this stores water, which may be evaporated from the soil and lost through the stomata of plants as transpiration. This evapo-transpiration provides cooling, which immediately reduces the transfer of heat into the building. This effect has been clearly demonstrated in Chicago, where the thermal performances of City Hall (which has a green roof) and Cook County Hall (with a conventional roof) are continuously monitored. On hot summer days, the effect of the green roof is to slow down the warming of the building in the morning, to reduce peak temperatures and to accelerate cooling in the late afternoon. The maximum air temperature difference above the green roof and the conventional roof is 9°C. This cooling has a significant effect on the interior temperature on the upper floors of City Hall and savings in air-conditioning costs are reported to be $5000 per annum.[35] The National

Research Council in Canada has compared a 150 mm deep green roof with a conventional roof and found that the green roof reduced the energy demand for cooling by 75% – equivalent to 6.0 kWh/m^2/day.[36] In various studies the reduction in summer midday temperature in rooms beneath green roofs, when compared with similar rooms without green roofs, has been shown to be between 5°C and 7°C.[37,38] It seems that green roofs really do work in terms of keeping buildings cooler in summer.

Green Roofs, Rainwater Attenuation and Cooling

For any given green roof substrate (growing medium), the greater the depth, the greater its water holding capacity. An extensive green roof is a low-maintenance roof where low growing vegetation is usually left to reach its own equilibrium. A typical extensive green roof with 100 mm of substrate absorbs about 50% of the rainfall that falls upon it each year and this water provides valuable evaporative cooling (see figure 9.11). The deeper substrates of intensive green roofs (roof gardens) absorb even more rain and provide even more evaporative cooling. Thermal imaging and detailed studies by Marco Schmidt and his colleagues at the Technical University of Berlin, shows how temperatures soar on exposed roofs and walls, but stay close to ambient temperature where substrate and vegetation facilitate cooling.[39] The ability of green roofs to absorb rainwater is not only useful in terms of providing evapo-transpirative cooling but is also a useful source

Type of green roof	Substrate depth (mm)	Typical vegetation	Water retention as % of annual rainfall
Extensive	20-40	Sedum	40
	40-60	Sedum	45
	60-100	Sedum, herbs	50
	100-150	Sedum, herbs, grass	55
	150-200	Herbs, grass	60
Intensive	200-250	Lawns, shrubs	60
	250-500	Lawns, shrubs	70
	>500	Lawns, shrubs, trees	90+

Figure 9.11 Annual rainwater absorption of various green roofs.[40]

129

control mechanism in sustainable drainage systems, where the purpose is to reduce the speed and volume of surface water runoff following heavy rainfall. In the absence of green roofs, rainfall quickly enters drains and can overwhelm drainage systems, causing localised flooding. Even when local drains and streams can cope, the sudden pulse of water can cause scouring or erosion and result in losses of biodiversity or flooding downstream. Green roofs can combine with rainwater harvesting and other sustainable drainage techniques to reduce or eliminate these problems; indeed, they can be so effective that it is possible to build zero-discharge developments, where for all but the most extreme weather events no surface water flows from the site, reducing the need for investment in expensive conventional drainage.

Green Roofs Need the Right Substrate

For a wide range of benefits to be realised from the use of green roofs – increased comfort, improved microclimate, better thermal performance and slower drainage – it is recommended that sufficient quantity of substrate is used to absorb water. In practice, ultra-lightweight green roof systems tend to dry out rapidly in summer and therefore a minimum substrate depth of 100 mm is recommended in temperate climates and an even greater depth in arid places. In addition, it is advantageous to use special green roof substrate mixtures that have been devised to be lightweight, but have a high capacity to absorb water and are also free draining. Organic materials do absorb water well, but they should also be limited at roof level, where irrigation is not provided, because they dry and decay and are easily blown away. German guidance recommends that organic material in green roof substrates does not exceed 20% by weight, because large quantities of organic material also constitute a fire risk when dry.[41]

Green Roofs for Biodiversity

The most important objective in the management of the environment must be the maintenance of biodiversity and the habitats that support it, because without this we cannot survive. Buildings, and in particular green roofs, can play a valuable role in providing habitat, especially for invertebrates and birds. Buildings are also important as roost and hibernation sites for bats. Where the strength of the building structure is adequate and the soil depth is sufficient, a wide range of vegetation can be grown, including trees and shrubs and it is even possible to establish ponds and other wetland features on roofs. Ayako Nagase and her colleagues at the Chiba University in Japan have described how green roofs are increasingly being used to provide wildlife habitat in their country.[42] Buildings strengthened to withstand earthquakes have the necessary strength to bear the weight of substrates that may be 500 mm or more in depth. At her 10th floor study site, which received no maintenance for eight years, a wide range of predominantly native trees and shrubs have been planted. Although not all trees thrive in 500 mm of substrate, some do, and the extra habitat provided by shaded leaf litter complements pond features and other wildflower areas more typical of green roofs. The creation of extensive roofs designed for biodiversity was pioneered in Switzerland by Stephan Brenneisen. In the 1990s he had become concerned with the loss of Rhineland alluvial grassland habitat and was aware that the invertebrate fauna associated with such grassland was finding refuge on brownfield sites in the city of Basel. Green roofs were already a statutory requirement in new developments in Switzerland at that time, but Brenneisen began to investigate how green roofs could be modified or designed to provide suitable habitat for invertebrates. His concern was that where new development was to proceed on brownfield sites, invertebrate populations would be lost. Brenneisen sought to determine whether or not green roofs could provide appropriate and meaningful mitigation for such impacts. He therefore undertook surveys of beetles and spiders on 16 green roofs in Basel, with the results published in 2002.[43] He recorded 172 species of beetles, 10% of which were listed in the national Red Data Book. His study on spiders revealed that 40% of the collected species were of 'faunistic interest' (a term used in the German speaking countries to indicate rarity). His study concluded that there were a number of factors that influenced the composition of invertebrate assemblages on green roofs, the most important of which was variation in substrate depth. Areas of thin substrate, which tend to be bare or sparsely vegetated, were found to provide suitable habitat for a number of drought-tolerant invertebrates. Deeper areas of substrate, however, retained more moisture and supported more vegetation, which had the effect of creating habitat mosaics that were able to support other invertebrate assemblages. The results of his research have led to changes in Cantonal Law in Basel, which requires roofs to be topographically varied in order to promote invertebrate diversity (see figure 9.12). Wherever possible, seeding with a mixture of local drought-tolerant wildflowers is used to accelerate colonisation by invertebrates.

London's Black Redstart Roofs

Brenneisen's work in Switzerland was an inspiration for Dusty Gedge in London, who was similarly concerned with the lost of brownfield habitats, but in his case the main species of concern was the black redstart. This bird, which is rare in England, colonised the rubble of

Figure 9.12 Green roofs created for biodiversity in Basel, Switzerland.

bombsites after World War II and still persists on derelict post-industrial sites. Gedge successfully campaigned for the creation of biodiverse roofs in London for the black redstart and other wildlife – named as 'brown roofs' because they replicated conditions on brownfield sites. Gedge's efforts encouraged Richard Jones, Gyongyver Kadas and others to undertake research over a period of several years, which confirmed the importance of green roofs in London for the conservation of invertebrates and also confirmed the value of varying substrate depth, using a range of wildflowers and including habitat features such as logs. This is the reason why roofs should not, as a matter of course, be covered with uniform swards of sedum, the predominant extensive green roof type.

Biodiverse Green Roofs in North America

In North America, green roof experts are also applying their knowledge of ecological restoration and permaculture to the establishment of vegetation on buildings, using locally appropriate palettes of native species. Examples of this approach may be seen on the California Academy of Sciences in San Francisco, which has achieved LEED Platinum. (LEED,[44] or Leadership in Energy and Environmental Design, is the internationally recognised green building certification system,

Figure 9.13 The ACROS Building, Fukuoka, Japan.

equivalent to BREEAM[45] or the Code for Sustainable Homes in the UK). Paul Kephart and colleagues at Rana Creek have advised on the Vancouver Convention Centre Extension, where the intention is to attract butterflies and hummingbirds to a 2.4 hectares living roof. [46]

Roof Gardens for People

Where inaccessible extensive green roofs are created, with the necessary guidance it is relatively straightforward to create wildlife habitat; however, on roof gardens (intensive green roofs), where there is an emphasis on access and enjoyment and where regular maintenance is expected and is easy to arrange, there may be different expectations. Aesthetic considerations may come to the fore, and on large commercial residential or institutional buildings, like architect Emilio Ambasz's ACROS Building in Fukuoka, Japan (see figure 9.13), the plantings may resemble those of a park or garden more than a nature reserve. The terraces on the roof of the ACROS Building are fully accessible and in effect extend the adjacent public park without compromising the function of the building as a conference hall and performance centre. No matter how formal or busy a roof garden is, however, the thermal, drainage and biodiversity functions should not be forgotten. It is possible to provide formality and to combine the requirements of visitors with those of wildlife by using the principles of ecological restoration and referring to the experience gained in places like Chibu, Basel and Vancouver.

Worldwide Applications

Roof gardens have a long history, having been included on palaces and citadels in the Renaissance (like those created by the Gonzaga family in Mantua, Italy) and probably long before that. In Europe, modern

133

green roofs also have a long history, with guidance promulgated by the German Landscape Research Development and Construction Society (FLL) as long ago as 1984, so there is confidence in Europe, and increasingly in North America in industry-standard technology and methods, but as the idea spreads across the globe there is a need to develop new methods of vegetating buildings. Basic components such as waterproofing may be suitable all over the globe, but each climate and bioregion should develop locally appropriate substrates and planting strategies so that the performance of each green roof is tuned to suit its setting and so that benefits for local biodiversity are maximised. This means that research on locally appropriate green roof substrates and plants will be undertaken all over the globe as the technology spreads. There is already evidence of this happening, with research underway in universities and other institutions in several countries representing a wide range of climates including Australia, Brazil, China, Greece, Iran, New Zealand, Singapore and Turkey. In China, for example, the green roof and living wall industries are already thriving. Living walls were particularly visible at the World Expo in Shanghai in 2010.[47] Singapore is leading the way in developing tropical building-integrated vegetation and celebrates this with the term 'skyrise greenery'.[48]

Wildlife and Buildings

Some wildlife has learnt to live in close association with people and their homes and places of work in the last few millennia. There are pests like rats and mice, of course, but also harmless creatures, including several species of bat and birds such as the swift, swallow and house martin. In recent decades as older buildings have been demolished or refurbished, there has been a tendency to close off openings and voids, thus depriving wildlife of nesting and roosting sites. Building standards have improved and there is a desire to make buildings airtight, which means that new buildings have usually lacked the beneficial nooks and crannies found in older buildings (although they do often include ledges, which act as perches for pests such as feral pigeons). In concert with the loss of roosting and nesting sites, modern cities have become tidier, with fewer wild plants and less insect prey for birds and bats. This has caused a decline in numbers – with some species such as the house sparrow suffering a huge decline – a 66% fall in London between 1995 and 2007.[49] More than 60 species of bird are known to use artificial nest boxes, which can, and should, be included on, or even in the fabric of, buildings. Bird boxes for particular species can be manufactured to designs provided by various expert groups, or even purchased from specialist manufacturers like Schwegeler.[50,51] Advice should be sought on suitable locations for boxes – some birds prefer certain heights and aspects, and exposed boxes may put the young at risk from high temperatures or predators. Purpose-made boxes manufactured from untreated timber or a cement and woodchip mixture are available for bats. Several species are known to use them both for roosting and breeding. Roosting boxes should be placed in sunny locations out of the reach of predators. Other, normally larger, well-insulated boxes, which can help create conditions of stable temperatures and humidity, are also available for use as hibernation sites. Experts caution that boxes are not able to substitute for all kinds of natural tree holes or voids in buildings but they do have a role in helping to replace roosts and hibernation sites lost through development and refurbishment.[52] For those who require further detailed information on how to attract wildlife to buildings, excellent guidance is available from nature conservation and green building bodies.[53] Ground-nesting birds are also attracted to large extensive green roofs. Most extensive green roofs are free from human disturbance and inaccessible to predators such as cats and foxes. They also have a wide horizon, which makes them ideal for ground-nesting birds, which avoid sites with overlooking trees, which could provide perches for birds of prey. Examples of extensive green roofs with nesting birds include the Rolls Royce factory near Goodwood, Sussex, which has supported three pairs of skylarks, and roofs on distribution centres at Emmen in Luzern, Switzerland where lapwing are a regular feature. In Emmen, initial problems with chick mortality have been solved by expert Natalie Baumann, who has added shelters, shallow pools and other habitat features.[54]

Figure 9.14 Rooftop permaculture, Florida, USA.

Rooftop Harvests

Sir Benjamin Ward Richardson, a prominent physician, anaesthetist and sanitarian, founded the Journal of Public Health in 1855 and was an early advocate of the benefits of cycling. Writing in 1876, he argued that in all large towns the roof of each house should be a garden.[55] He believed that widespread creation of roof gardens would result in a vast increase in the health and the happiness of the population. Now nearly 140 years later, in Brooklyn, New York, Ben Flanner is making rooftop gardening his livelihood by growing 30 or more varieties of fresh vegetables, herbs and fruit for the many restaurants in the neighbourhood.[56] The advantage of this kind of enterprise is that fresh, high-quality produce can be delivered to the customer within minutes of harvest. This kind of initiative brings the usual benefits of roof greening to the building – intercepting rainfall and providing summer cooling, but the installation pays for itself and there is no maintenance bill as there would be for an ornamental garden. Pioneers like Kevin Songer in Florida are also demonstrating that rooftop vegetable gardening is feasible in sub-tropical locations (see figure 9.14).[57] Clearly there is a future for rooftop farming along with the whole range of other possibilities that I have described. Building exteriors should not ordinarily be naked, but should be made to work harder for interior comfort, for the benefit of people and wildlife and to conserve the wider environment.

10. Conclusion

When many dream together it is the beginning of a new reality

– Friedensreich Hundertwasser

Interesting Times

Civilisation and cities are at a turning point in history. The remarkable growth of population, which was triggered by the Enlightenment, gathered pace during the Industrial Revolution and accelerated during the 20th century, is set to level off during the coming decades, in concert with the peak in oil supplies and other resources. The global climate is changing as the result of emissions of greenhouse gases and experts are predicting a sea level rise, more floods and more droughts. The agriculture that is necessary to feed the cities has spread across virtually all landscapes that are capable of sustaining it (and some that are not). Rivers have been polluted and channelised, wetlands drained, forests felled and the seas plundered for fish and filled with trash. We are also in the midst of a precipitous loss in biodiversity that is unprecedented during the life of our own species. Solving these problems is not just about cities – we need to secure clean and safe supplies of energy and water. Farming and industry must now begin their transition to the post peak oil era, which will involve changes in direction towards an ecological approach with a move towards closed-loop processes. Inevitably most of the restoration

Ecosystem Services Come to Town: Greening Cities by Working with Nature,
First Edition. Gary Grant.
© 2012 John Wiley & Sons, Ltd. Published 2012 by John Wiley & Sons, Ltd.

of biodiversity will occur outside of cities, in the oceans, forests, steppes, deserts and farms. However, cities must play their part because most of humanity now lives in cities. Cities occupy only a fraction of the territory used for farming (cities occupy about 2% of the land surface of the world); however, certain cities do sprawl across large areas. Cities also consume resources and pollute the wider environment. The polluted runoff from cities can damage the longest rivers and reach the centres of our oceans. Existing cities are inefficient, dry, hotter than their hinterlands and relatively barren. Business as usual is no longer a wise option.

The Positives

There are many aspects of our cities that we must celebrate of course. Most cities include buildings and precincts of great beauty and they are all centres of culture, knowledge and learning. We can conserve and reproduce the best elements from the past. Nature does thrive here and there in our city parks, gardens or in neglected corners. This has often occurred by accident or by neglect, but we can, with some ease if we have the mind to, deliberately increase the biodiversity in our cities. There are now many examples of city greening – enough to clearly demonstrate how our city problems can be solved. Communities are beginning to plan their city regions to promote the movement of people and wildlife. Cities and regions are collaborating in the management of watersheds. Nations are collaborating in the management of great rivers, lakes and seas.

Cities and Citizens Take the Initiative

Professional people from all sectors, including health and energy, as well as engineering, planning and architecture, are beginning to collaborate more effectively, increasingly united by the concepts of sustainability and resilience in the face of the crises we face. These partners will be even more effective if they align their work with nature and work towards the conservation, restoration and maintenance of ecosystems. Reports and studies are produced, and governments ponder and prevaricate, but cities and citizens do not need to wait for national governments to legislate or pronounce in order to act. Jurisdictions are cooperating to make regional and city-wide initiatives a reality, including the preservation and restoration of ecological corridors, green wedges and green belts. Open spaces are increasingly being designed and managed to be multi-functional – to store floods, to slow and clean surface water runoff, to provide routes for cycling and walking, to provide habitat for wildlife or to grow food. Networks

Figure 10.1 Rogner Therme at Bad Blumau, Austria by Hundertwasser.

Figure 10.2 Green building and active transportation, London.

of green space are now classified as green infrastructure and are given economic as well as aesthetic value. Neighbourhood green spaces are also being promoted as essential for physical and mental health. The shade of trees and the moisture in the soil have been clearly demonstrated to be an effective and economical solution to the overheating associated with urban heat islands. Citizens with no technical training often seem to instinctively know how to get the most from their own patch, and more needs to be done to involve people in the design and maintenance of neighbourhoods.

Greening Requires Greenery

Now, even the buildings themselves can be used to capture the energy of the wind and sun. However, in my opinion, a high standard of energy efficiency alone is no longer enough for a building to be considered 'green'. Rainwater that falls on buildings is too precious to be sent straight to drains, and should be used to support plants or stored for reuse. Buildings can provide ecosystem services too, by supporting soil and vegetation, which has been shown to reduce the energy consumption as well as improving the local microclimate. These concepts suggest that there will be a new direction for architecture that will stimulate further innovation. This will be accelerated by new ways of collaborating and thinking, but we do not need to wait for such changes in order to begin the green transformation of our cities – transformations that will be necessary if we are to successfully adapt to climate change and to reverse environmental degradation and biodiversity losses. All the necessary techniques, skills and knowledge already exist, whether they are related to sensitivity to water, capture of energy or establishment of vegetation. Remember that a city, neighbourhood or building isn't truly green without water, soil, vegetation and wildlife. I believe that citizens are willing and able to work together to make this simple and effective vision a reality.

I: award winning projects from IHDC website

"We the mayors and governors of the world's leading cities.... Ask you to recognize that the future of our globe will be won or lost in the cities of the world."
– Copenhagen Climate Change communiqué, December 2009

Mission Earth

In 2005, after five years of work by ecologists and environmental scientists around the world, the Millennium Ecosystem Assessment was published. It confirmed that every one of the Earth's major ecosystems was in decline. Species and habitat loss was occurring at an alarming rate and that, if we continued to use up natural resources at current rates, our natural life support system would not be able to sustain human life beyond 2050.

In 2008, for the first time, more than half the world's population was living in towns and cities and in 2009, the 9th Summit of the UN Convention of the Parties (COP) on Climate Change in Copenhagen made the statement that "the future of our globe will be won or lost in the cities of the world".

This was the background, in 2009, when the instigators of the Integrated Habitats Design Competition, Gary Grant, Dusty Gedge and Blanche Cameron, realised that there is now a real opportunity for ecologists, architects, landscape architects, engineers, surveyors, planners, developers, insurers, investors, contractors, clients and communities to use ecological knowledge to transform our built environment in order to restore nature, adapt to climate change and to provide a long-term future for humanity.

Transforming the Way We Think about the Built Environment

Traditionally, however, the built environment professions have not tended to work in close communication, leading to calls for us to get out of our silos and work more closely together to share knowledge, skills, ideas and lessons learnt across the built environment disciplines. Our urban areas and landscapes have an impact on the wider environment which must be reduced. However they are also experiencing more chaotic and intense weather – including more intense rainstorms, increased periods of drought, hotter urban heat islands, poor air and water quality, and loss of the biodiversity on which we all rely.

Ecosystem Services Come to Town: Greening Cities by Working with Nature,
First Edition. Gary Grant.
© 2012 John Wiley & Sons, Ltd. Published 2012 by John Wiley & Sons, Ltd.

To date, the language of green design has tended to focus on 'minimising our negative impacts on the environment'. This is such a poor ambition, given both the scale of the problem and the huge potential of humanity to respond to challenges of design, communication and collaborative action. What is required is a restorative, ecosystem approach that puts nature at the heart of what we do – and in turn provides us with the essential ecosystem services that we rely on for life.

Multifunctional Design

The Integrated Habitats Design Competition (IHDC) challenges conventional design thinking, calling for creative, restorative development approaches that demonstrate how designing for nature and the ecosystem services it provides improves conditions for ourselves: cooling the urban heat island, filtering air and water, managing storm water and flash flooding, supporting nature with the habitats, forage and shelter it needs, and providing biodiverse green spaces for people to benefit from and enjoy.

International Inspirations

Around the world ecological knowledge is being applied by built environment professionals. For example, The American Society of Landscape Architects encourages its members to plan and design each project in order to provide ecosystem services. Australian cities have adopted water sensitive urban design, which has the provision of ecosystem services at its core. Cities in the US such as Philadelphia, Portland, Seattle and New York have been initiating community-led green infrastructure approaches that empower local people to manage issues of storm water, biodiversity restoration and urban greening in their own neighbourhoods.

In 2007, Metro Portland organised an international competition, Integrating Habitats (http://www.integratinghabitats.org). This competition asked entrants to design for locally-appropriate species, with features that should be integrated into the heart of each development. Three categories asked designers to present ideas for mixed use development and riparian forest, retail development and lowland forest, neighbourhood infill and oak woodland. The results were inspirational to us as founders of the IHDC.

The IHDC Brief

The IHDC offers opportunities for entrants to propose designs – either creative ideas or as-built projects – for any urban site, with any use and of any scale. However it must demonstrate how the development supports nature, by relating to local and national Biodiversity Action Plans and integrating locally appropriate biodiverse green infrastructure and habitats for nature conservation.

Participants are also asked to demonstrate the benefits of this approach, in terms of terms of cooling the urban heat island, surface water management, water and air filtration, energy demand reduction, micro climate and neighbourhood benefits.

These criteria also respond to broader concerns reflected in European Directives and other similar regulations on biodiversity, water and flood management, and air quality, as well as longer-term issues of resource depletion and fossil fuel use.

Unusual Partnerships

Key to the IHDC process has been the embodiment of an interdisciplinary process that puts the provision of ecosystem services at its core. A judging board was developed with representatives from across the disciplines – ecologists, architects, engineers, campaigners, academics, regulators and policy makers.

Co-instigators Gary Grant (Chair) and Dusty Gedge were joined as judges by Brian McDonald from Natural England and Paul Shaffer, water specialist at CIRIA, Dr Jean Venables, Past President of the Institution of Civil Engineers, Martin Hunt at Forum for the Future, Phil Baarda at Scottish Natural Heritage, Peter Massini from the Greater London Authority, Alice Tree from the Scottish EPA, John Day from the RSPB, Dr Lisa Hundt at the Bat Conservation Trust, Paul Collins from Nottingham Trent University and architects Justin Bere and Andy Simmonds.

Natural England has championed the IHDC since the beginning, as part of their Natural Development process. The IHDC conferences, exhibitions and award ceremonies have been supported by prominent public institutions such as the Museum of London, as part of their work to install 4,200 square metres of biodiverse green roofs and other green infrastructure, and the Natural History Museum, led by Dr Bob Bloomfield, Head of Innovation and co-ordinator of the UK Friends of the UN Decade on Biodiversity 2011– 2020. Government departments have also shown their support, in the form of the Green Infrastructure Partnership, supported by Defra and the DCLG.

Importantly, support has also come from the business sector – from developers Kier, and from the Victoria Business Improvement District, relating to their pioneering Green Infrastructure Audit undertaken by Land Use Consultants with support from the Green Roof Consultancy.

Case Studies – Creating a Body of Exemplar Projects

The IHDC receives entries from commercial, academic and community teams, with a range of projects including single buildings, mixed-use developments and masterplanning scale approaches.

It is building a body of work that envisages how the UK could adopt an ecosystem services approach to planning, designing, installing and managing our built environment.

Entrants have not always embraced the brief entirely. Some proposals have focused purely on biodiversity restoration (albeit in an expert and ecologically appropriate way) but without the urban context. Others have prioritised specific climate change adaptation and resilience issues such as energy demand reduction or food growing, but without sufficiently exploring ways of also benefitting biodiversity.

However, the winners and finalists that follow show some of the multifunctional approaches and ideas that the competition has evoked, where nature is prioritised, and at the same time demonstrating the benefits that flow from this approach for humans too.

IHDC Case Studies

Edge Hill Halls of Residence, Liverpool
Maria Cristina Banceanu
IHDC 2010 Winner

Project Overview

This project takes an abandoned rail depot area and transforms it into student halls of residence, which is designed to attract wildlife through habitats integrated into both the building fabric and in the spaces on and around the buildings.

The halls of residence are equipped with the latest energy and resource conservation technology. Rainwater is collected in a reservoir and filtered through a sand bed system, waste water from the housing is channeled through a septic tank and reed bed system, eventually feeding into a wildlife lake. Noise and general pollution to the flats is reduced by a bund area raised around the entire site. Vegetation selected for the site is local and requires little maintenance.

The greenhouse is obtained by enclosing the former rail depot and collecting the rainwater falling upon it. All accommodation units have biodiverse green roofs or green terraces. Swift and swallow nesting boxes are integrated into the facades of the buildings. The canteen provides a space for owls in its roof structure. Corridors are ventilated by tall ventilation chimneys equipped with bat boxes at their top.

Judges' Comments

"This entrant really did engage with the brief giving attention to local species of plants and biodiversity issues. This approach did not compromise the wider issues of sustainability addressed in the scheme, showing an impressive combination of clever site planning with attention to detail. There is practical integration of energy efficiency, water conservation and biodiversity features. The judges were charmed by the thoughtful inclusion of space for bats and birds."

MARIA-CRISTINA
BANCEANU
UNIVERSITY OF LIVERPOOL
SCHOOL OF ARCHITECTURE
PROJECT: EDGE HILL HALLS LIVERPOOL

EDGE HILL HALLS

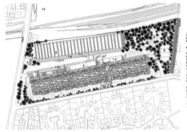

1 BUSS / CAR ENTRANCE
2 BUSS CAR EXIT
3 UNDERGROUND CAR PARK ENTRANCE
4 SECURITY LODGE & BIKE SHELTER
5 GREENHOUSE
6 BAR & CANTINE
7 SEPTIC SYSTEM
8 RECREATION AREA
9 TENNIS COURTS
10 UNDERGROUND CAR PARK EXIT
11 ACCOMMODATION AREA
12 HALLS CONNECTION
13 SOUTHERN VIEW &
14 THE BUND
15 LOCAL MEDICAL CLINIC
15 HALLS RECEPTION
16 LAKE & REED BED
17 SAND FILTERS &
18 COMPOST BINS
18 RESERVOIR
19 CAR PARK

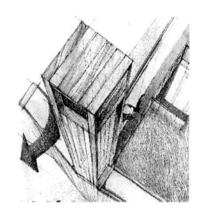

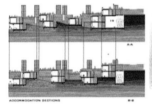

THE SITE:
FORMER EDGE HILL DEPOT & JUNK CAR YARD

ACCOMMODATION SECTIONS

HOUSING DETAILS
TIMBER
STRUCTURE

VIEW TOWARDS ONE OF THE MANY COURTYARDS

1 ENTRANCE
2 RECEPTION AREA
3 RECEPTIONIST VESTIBUL
4 LAUNDRY AREA
5 TOILETS
6 COMMON ROOM
7 LIBRARY
8 MUSIC ROOM
9 COMPUTER ROOM
10 ADMINISTRATOR OFFICE
11 KITCHEN 1
12 STAIRS
13 RESERVOIR
14 ENTRANCE TO UNDERGROUND CAR-PARK

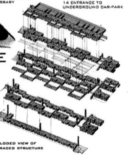

THE SCHEME
CATERED ACCOMMODATION FOR
558 STUDENTS & 18 TUTORS

ADDITIONAL SIMPLE STRUCTURE
TRANSFORMS THE DEPOT INTO A
GREENHOUSE WITH RAINWATER
COLLECTING SYSTEM

EXPLODED VIEW OF
TERRACED STRUCTURE

BIODIVERSITY

SWALLOW & SWIFT HOUSES

SPECIALLY DESIGNED
INLETS BETWEEN FACADE
FRAMES FOR NESTING
BOXES

DOUBLE TANK SEPTIC
SYSTEM & REED BED
SYSTEM:
INCOMING WASTE WATER FILTERED
BY SEPTIC TANK, PUMPED TO THE
RESERVOIR. FLOATING REED BED
CLEANS SEWAGE, VIABLE FOR
UNDERWATER LIFE, EVEN FISHING

VENTILATION CHIMNEYS &
BAT BOXES:
USE OF STACK EFFECT PROVIDES
CORRIDOR AIR EXCHANGE AND WARMS
BAT BOXES LOCATED AT TOP OF
CHIMNEYS. ALL LOCATED IN ABOVE
GROUND LEVEL.

VERTICAL GARDENS &
NATIVE VEGETATION

VERTICAL GARDENS
TO BE LOCATED ON
EXTERIOR CORRIDOR
WALLS

PLANTS REQUIRED:
TREES: RHUS TYPHINA
WILDFLOWERS: OXEYE
DAISY, RED CLOVER,
COLTSFOOT, GREATER KNAPWEED
(TO BE PLANTED ON ROOFS AND THE
BUND)

SAND FILTERS & RESERVOIR
PURIFY RESERVOIR
WATER BEFORE BEING
USED IN THE HOMES.
RESERVOIR DEPTH:2H
CAPACITY: 4610 m³

THE BUND
MAN MADE EARTHSTRUCTURE
FROM EXCAVATED SOIL
SURROUNDS SITE PROVIDING THE
BASIN FOR DRAINING RAINWATER
AND SOUND & POLLUTION
BARRIER FROM ADJACENT
RAILWAY AND ROADS

ROOF VIEW:
3.60 m² SOLAR PANNELS PER EACH SINGLE
ROOM
ZENITHAL VESTIBULE LIGHTING: 4.5 m² PER
EACH 2 PERSON FLAT
ZENITHAL CORRIDOR LIGHTING
GREEN ROOF: 22.4m² PER EACH 2 PERSON
FLAT, SOME TRANSFORMED IN GREEN
TERRACES

OWL SPACE - CANTINE ROOF

GROWING MEDIUM
DEPTH DEPENDS ON PLANTING
3-6 MM CRUSHED GRAVEL
FILTER FLEECE
WATER RETAINING PLASTIC TRAY
FIBRE PROTECTION MAT (ROOT BARRIER)
SEPARATION LAYER
SINGLE PLY WATERPROOF MEMBRANE
VAPOUR BARRIER
THERMAL INSULATION 100 TO 300 MM
ROOF DECKING
TRUSSED INNER FAKE ROOF
(SPACE FOR CLEANING OWL SPACE)
TRAP DOOR LEADING TO OWL SPACE
OWL SPACE

Matripolis, Tyneside
David Dobereiner and Paul Jones
IHDC 2010 Runner Up

Project Overview

This scheme is designed house 500 people in a compact, sustainable development on a terraced slope, such that everyone can step directly from their front door into a rich realm of biodiversity. The scheme is intended to respect all species, living together in an integrated landscape, which encourages nature to thrive, and hopefully encourage species, which are currently largely extinct in the area, to return the Northeast.

The proposal is on the banks of the Tyne on the site of the old Swan Hunter shipyard. The site was once a bustling community but is now derelict. The proposal hopes to reintroduce a sense of community by integrating living and working.

The project reconsiders the terraced housing typology that was ubiquitous in the northeast in the last century. Terraces are stepped up the hill from a public square where community facilities that contribute to a sense of place are located. The second tier contains work units for light industry, to support the community as a whole.

The facility is carbon-negative and uses environmentally beneficial materials. Energy is generated from hydro-turbines located in the river. The scheme is a passive design, to avoid the need for heating or cooling. Food for the residents is grown in the allotment gardens and greenhouses. Access through the community is via staircases and wildlife corridors as well as a lightweight pedestrian and bike ramp connecting all residents to common spaces and services at grade level.

Judges' Comments

"Transforming an old brownfield site, this team effort addresses the issues of biodiversity in urban developments whilst also addressing the needs of the human animal! This is an impressive proposal which shows how biodiversity could be introduced into even the most compact of urban areas by deliberately creating interconnected multi-level networks of wildlife habitat."

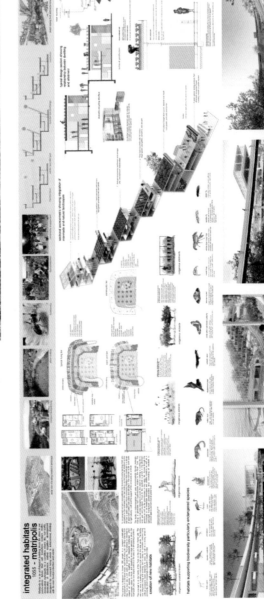

The Seed Catalogue: Ecological regeneration planning tool
Team R_E_D: Susannah Hagan, Mark Gaterell and Silvio Caputo
IHDC 2010 Highly Commended

Project Overview

The Seed Catalogue is a way of systematising and implementing an ecological intensification of struggling post-industrial cities. It relies on the power of the 'growing' to bring measurable environmental and economic benefits to its users, and consists of a series of economically and/or environmentally productive 'tiles', with rules for applying each of them to different kinds of urban open spaces.

Choice of tiles would vary with different cities, but the strategy is transferable to any city with a combination of unused open spaces and low land values. The tiles can proliferate as ventures succeed, joining separate open spaces into one regenerative 'bio-economic' system. Instead of wild nature taking over brownfield sites, husbanded nature does: orchards, reed beds, hedgerows. Instead of the city's wastes being exported, and energy imported, they are handled in situ by 'artificial ecosystems'.

We propose another approach to regenerating declining UK cities, which accepts the reality of populations too small for a city's physical size, a shrinking tax base and rock bottom land values, and which sees these as opportunities rather than as signs of decay.

We propose that cities unable to make the transition to a post-industrial economy as well as some of their competitors could place themselves in the forefront of a different kind of urban regeneration – grown, not built – which could create small businesses, and increase employment and tax revenue.

We propose *The Seed Catalogue*. This is literally about seeds (planting organic market gardens, wildflowers for beekeeping, trees) – and about seed money (small capital investments to grow businesses in blighted communities).

Judges' Comments

"Conceptually a very interesting proposal as long as it is applied in a locally appropriate way to ecosystem services and biodiversity. A powerful and original idea that could really make planning for vacant sites more interesting and engaging. This could really catch on."

INTEGRATED HABITATS - THE SEED CATALOGUE

R_E_D

The Seed Catalogue: The Seed Catalogue is the engine of the strategy, demonstrating the array of options available to cities with degraded open spaces. Each option has rules governing its deployment. These relate to size of site (eg commercially viable?), type of climate (eg enough rainfall to grow what?), surrounding context (houses? commercial?), soil condition (polluted, paved over?), and economic condition (some public money available for investment? zone?). These rules allow users to choose which tiles in the Seed Catalogue are most appropriate for their city. The specific content of these tiles – eg types of trees planted for 'habitat', types of fruit for 'income' – would vary with the climate and soil of the city in question.

HABITAT	INCOME	METABOLISM	ENERGY

The Seed Catalogue In Evolution

The Catalogue tiles can, over time, join up into one regenerative 'bio-economic' system. In this, organic produce (for which demand currently outstrips supply), habitat, metabolic servies, and increasing community employment, combine to form an overlay of 'ecological enterprise' on the existing urban fabric, which benefits both citizens and biregion.

phase 1

phase 2

phase 3

149

Happy Habitats, Bath
Buro Happold and Grant Associates: Laura Crawford, Phil Hampshire,
Aylin Ludwig, Tamasine Scott, Katherine Sydney,
Celia Way and Victoria Wilson
IHDC 2010 Finalist

Project Overview

"Happy Habitats" is a model that places nature and society at its heart – urban communities in which people can live, work and play alongside thriving natural systems.

The design process took three 'lenses': Food Production, Liveability and Urban Greening, to demonstrate the interaction between systems and features of the site and between biodiversity, ecosystems services, energy and carbon, water, economics and liveability.

Urban food production is a balancing act between space availability, substrate, access to water and sunlight. Therefore the "Happy Habitats" model encourages a philosophy of stacking, staggering and multifunctionality to optimise these aspects.

The model also aims, through liveability, to give people a sense of pride and belonging, encourage community involvement and connect inhabitants with their environment.

The Urban Greening lens emphasises the value of biodiverse green space and water systems, integrating habitats and enhancing the functionality and wellbeing of an urban area as a whole.

Judges' Comments

"This submission demonstrates that careful thought has been given to a number of complex interrelated issues. In approaching the project with a good philosophy, the team have been able to envisage a scheme that would combine functionality with a special waterside character. Could be less paving and more habitat but an interesting approach."

HAPPY HABITATS - where nature and society are at the very heart of the design

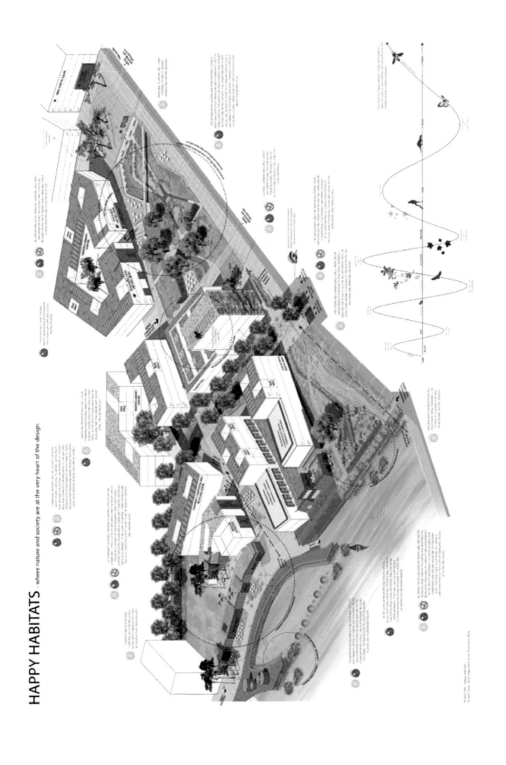

The Overflow Car Park, Hackney, London
Claire Mookerjee and Mat Triebner
IHDC 2010 Finalist

Project Overview

This proposal explores the possibility of a managed urban flood plain, and stresses the importance of multi-functional ecological infrastructure within the city.

We propose that working landscapes such as car parks, transport infrastructure and contaminated land are key to providing robust green infrastructure for the city. The discourse surrounding the city and second nature have often overstated landscapes of recreation. Here we re-imagine the way we surface our city to provide amenity, and imagine one that is *led* by landscape rather than one which simply incorporates it.

Based on the ridge and furrow formations of feudal land distribution patterns in the Middle Ages, our proposal mitigates storm water runoff and flooding within London, caused in part by groundwater mismanagement.

The design is a reinterpretation of the traditional car park, sited adjacent to a Tesco supermarket in central Hackney. It incorporates a series of hills and gullies to aid in groundwater management. The planted gullies and connected cisterns not only help to filter storm water and slow the rate at which it enters London's sewer system, but also create microhabitats for plants and animals.

Judges' Comments

"The judges were pleased to see an entrant tackle the important issue of water sensitivity and multi-functionality in urban design. The technical aspects need a little work but it is on the right track."

OVERFLOW CARPARK

HACKNEY, LONDON

Satoyama, City of London
Hiroyuki Ichihara and Atsumi Sako
IHDC 2010 Finalist

Project Overview

By 2007, around 36% of the bee colonies across Europe had been lost, due to Colony Collapse Disorder. Since one third of agricultural crops rely on cross-fertilisation, the problem is serious.

In response, this project aims to encourage bees back into the city and reintroduce the traditional act of 'honey hunting'.

'Satoyamas' or 'small green hills' can be integrated into living roofs to house hive boxes for rooftop bee keeping, as well as providing habitats for other types of bees. The human participants will be encouraged to visit these rooftop hives to take part in the collection of honey and therefore become directly involved with the local ecosystem.

The project aspires to create the necessary equipment to connect humans with nature through their own instinctive action. It also aims to regenerate unused 'niches' within the urban environment.

Judges' Comments

"This project shows real passion and innovation. The judges were impressed by the attention to the issue of seasonal changes and the city-wide approach to urban environmental problems through rooftop greening."

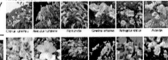

Over wrapping light onto city
Ancient Wisdom

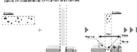

Global problem of CCD

Around 34% of bee colony over the Europe had been lost due to Colony Collapse disorder (CCD) on 2007. Since 1/3 of agricultural crops depend on cross fertilize, the problem is serious.

Diagram

■ Bee biology

■ Unused road

■ "Satoyama" structure

■ Management of honey

Carbon reduction Ro

Importance of bee in eco-system

Creation of "diet" involved eco-system

Ancient Wisdom

Japan has 4 seasons and Ancient people had various wisdom to overcome hot summer and freezing winter, using sunlight. "Chise" is a traditional house of Ainu, a minority ethnic in Japan. External wall of the house is made of bamboo grass leaves. In summer, leaves will be rolled backed by summer sunshine and block sunlight. In winter, snow will fall on leaves and make insulation. Also, daylight will spread by snow and enlighten the house. With only one outer covering, the space will optimized to accommodate surrounding environment by combination of character of seasons and daylight. "Wearing" natural phenomena, over wrapping nature of seasons and daylight onto outer covering, niches at cities will turn into new space with gathering people from negative space.

Regenerating city niches by light

Niches between buildings are forgotten from main street and rather negative places but accumulation space of wasted energy in cities at the same time. By over wrapping daylight and porous membrane, new space will be created.

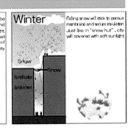

"Satoyama" on roof can activate nature relationship through bees. Also it can be spread over city through human "diet". People can bring this enjoyment of eating to their porch, balcony and street. Hedgehogs can move around marmalade green in city and green network will be spread from points to lines to creature's network.It can be a balanced ecosystem full of eating enjoyment. Relationship between human and nature connected by small insects and hedgehogs will draw children to happiness.

Over wrapping structure

- Winter: Snow
- Autumn: Fallen leaves
- Spring/Summer: Rain water
- water
- porous membrane
- Building
- Nearest city
- property

Controlling city environment with porous membrane, like Japanese used to control air flow seasonally by opening sliding screen or installing storm sash. Porous membrane can impound water and get air into city at the same time. Impounded water can change membrane into convex lens and spread daylight. Niches in city wrapped by porous membrane will change into new living space.

Porous membrane structure

Over wrapping seasonal light

Spring
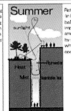
sunlight

Summer
sunlight

Autumn
sunlight

Winter
Snow

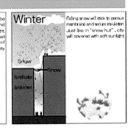

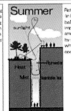

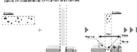

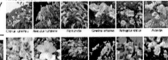

National Wildflower Centre, Knowsley, Liverpool
Landlife with Ian Simpson Architects and Hoare Lea Engineers: Grant Luscombe,
Ernst ter Horst, Julie Godefroy and Thomas Lefevre
IHDC 2010 Finalist

Project Overview

The National Wildflower Centre promotes awareness of wildflowers and new biodiverse habitats. This design – a collaboration between architects, sustainability engineers and structural engineers – expresses maths and physics theory through simple wildflower structures and natural phenomena.

A sweeping rammed earth wall draws visitors to a glazed entrance foyer. The main exhibition space is a single volume inspired by the symmetry of a flower head. Reflective 'petals' focus sunlight to create dazzling displays internally.

The proposals are designed to be carbon-neutral in operation and to achieve an 'Outstanding' BREEAM rating. High thermal insulation, natural ventilation and an 'earth duct' heat sink reduce energy demand, the remainder being met by harnessing on-site wind and solar power.

Judges' Comments

"This scheme will make a valuable addition to the National Wildflower Centre, enabling even more people to access and enjoy wildflowers and understand how biodiversity has a place in the urban environment."

NATIONAL WILDFLOWER CENTRE

URN: 1063

  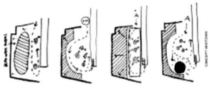

City Park, Hove Park, Brighton and Hove
Maria Hawton Mead with Jon Turner and Fergus Carr,
Turner Associates
IHDC 2010 Finalist

Project Overview

City Park is a new build site consisting of 7 low level residential units adjacent to Hove Park, and flanked on each side by new blocks of 3-storey flats overlooking the site.

The development is to be built to an exceptional level of sustainability, protecting and enhancing the existing biodiversity of the site. These buildings are adapted to cope with the changing climate and to minimise the 'heat island' effect.

The scale, style and sustainability of the site were key considerations: the scheme is largely single storey, with a curved chalk grassland green roof to link the single and smaller double storey elements in a sympathetic and organic form to its parkland setting. Green walls cover a high percentage of the total wall area.

The units achieve Code for Sustainable Homes Level 5 and Lifetime Homes Standards. They offer occupants an opportunity to live a low impact lifestyle alongside nature in the City of Brighton and Hove.

Judges' Comments

"The judges admired the elegant way that the green roof has been incorporated into a very well mannered scheme that would fit well into an existing residential neighbourhood."

City Park. Orchard Road. Hove

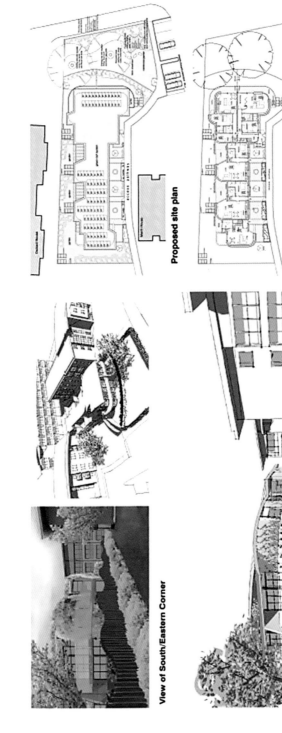

Side (Western) Elevation

Proposed site plan

Ground Floor

Lower Ground Floor

View of South/Eastern Corner

From Orchard Road / Orchard House

Shrubhill *Works*, Leith, Edinburgh
Michael Bryan
IHDC 2011 Winner

Project Overview

Shrubhill *Works* adapts a brownfield site to create a Cohousing community that encourages its residents to embrace a more sustainable lifestyle, forming a stronger bond with their surrounding natural environment and neighbours.

Communal facilities provide residents with access rather than ownership, reducing consumption and encouraging social interaction. The necessary organisational structures in this community will also benefit the development, and support monitoring of local endangered species and habitats.

Combined with the principles of Permaculture, the master plan is geared towards the provision of nature's 'goods and services' leading to an affordable, low impact, diverse place to live. Dwellings are designed to include passive green techniques, including solar buffers, natural ventilation and an on-site wastewater treatment plant, providing the site with grey water whilst simultaneously creating a new habitat.

Existing buildings on-site are renovated and retrofitted, reducing the impact on resources. The site also extends the region's wildlife corridors and sustainable transport networks through the adaptation of an adjacent railway line. Biodiversity within the site will be nurtured by large green spaces and designated wild areas, a bat spiral and beekeeping on the rooftop garden.

Judges' Comments

"The winning entry integrates community, energy, materials, water, food and biodiversity. It would transform a run-down inner city site into a water-sensitive urban village with permaculture at its heart.

Integration comes in the form of waste and wastewater treatment and rooftop gardens. The site includes plenty of wildlife habitat which links to the wider ecological network and species, including bats, birds and bees are catered for."

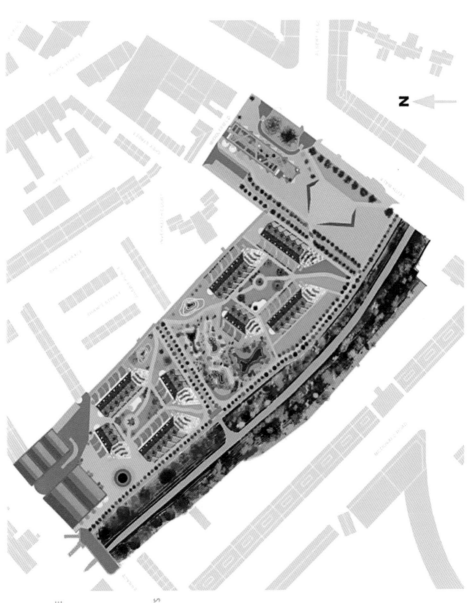

N

1. SHRUBHILL HOUSE COHOUSING APARTMENTS, ROOFTOP GARDEN & COMMUNAL FACILITIES

2. COMMUNITY MARKETPLACE & SQUARE

3. SITE BOUNDARY CAR-PARKING

4. CYCLE PATHS

5. SHRUBHILLWORKS COLONY COHOUSING

6. COMMUNITY GARDENS & ALLOTMENTS

7. LANDSCAPED HILLS CONTAINING WASTE WATER PRE-TREATMENT SEPTIC TANKS

8. ECOLOGICAL ON-SITE WASTE TREATMENT SYSTEM

9. MASONRY CHIMNEY STACK WITH BAT SPIRAL

10. RENOVATED WORKSHOP 1. - NEW COMMUNITY EDUCATION CENTRE

11. RENOVATED WORKSHOP 2. - COMMUNAL FACILITES FOR SHRUBHILLWORKS COHOUSING & COMBINED HEAT & POWER GENERATOR PROVIDING SITES ELECTRICITY SUPPLY & FEEDING DISTRICT HEATING SYSTEM

12. NEW EXTENSION TO EXISTING WILDLIFE CORRIDOR & CYCLE NETWORK

ROOFTOP GARDEN

WASTE WATER RECYCLING

Hafod Copperworks,
Swansea Lee Miles and Jennifer Acayan
IHDC 2011 Highly Commended

Project Overview

Hafod Copperworks aims to revive and regenerate a declining area of Swansea, through better integration with the natural environment.

Previously the site was a major copper works. Since the industrial decline of the area, the site remains polluted and damaged. However as numerous schemes gather pace to regenerate the nearby city of Swansea, to address socioeconomic problems, there is a real risk the biodiversity inherent in this site will be lost.

Through three themes of connection, conservation, and cultivation, this project proposes an integrated ecological regeneration scheme. These three thematic conceptual elements manifest throughout the project in the form of varying design interventions, applied to four distinct areas.

1   A residential suburb retrofitted with deployable elements such as biodiverse green roofs, modular greenhouses and solar panels. This will enable the community to gradually shift to a more sustainable lifestyle. This will also provide power and food.
2   A hilltop to be fitted with wind turbines. Agricultural areas will incorporate waste composting and anaerobic digestion.
3   New nature reserves which will be subject to improvement and better ecological management.
4   Restoration of central derelict factory into a valuable community hub for events and a local food market.

Judges' Comments

"A comprehensive masterplan designed to revive a contaminated post-industrial district associated with a former copper works with an emphasis on regeneration and connection with nature. The submission included a thorough analysis with impressive proposals for green infrastructure and green housing. This planning project goes beyond the scale envisaged by the judges, however it was commended for the ambitious way that it tackled complex greening issues throughout a whole district."

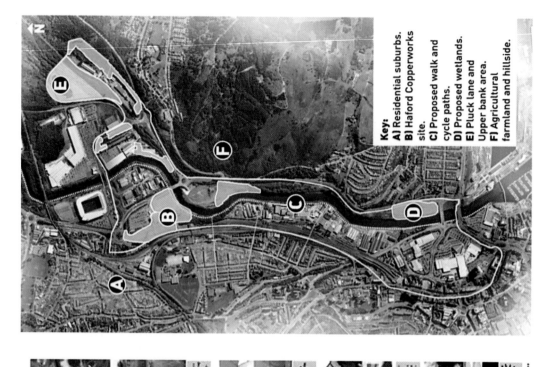

Key:
A) Residential suburbs.
B) Haford Copperworks site.
C) Proposed walk and cycle paths.
D) Proposed wetlands.
E) Pluck lane and Upper bank area.
F) Agricultural farmland and hillside.

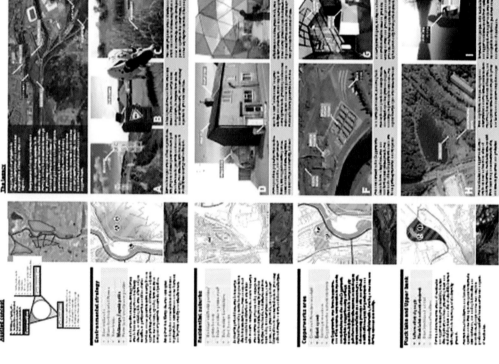

Swift Nesting Boxes, Holytown, Lanarkshire
Jackie Gilliland, Graeme Muir and Clare Darlaston with Concern
for Swifts (Scotland)
IHDC 2011 Highly Commended

Project Overview

This design for swift nest sites was developed through Concern for Swifts (Scotland) by North Lanarkshire Council architects. The design took the basic requirements for swift nest sites and developed this to fit into the shape and size of the eaves at the gable end of the building – where the original nest had been prior to refurbishment – and using the same materials as the new cladding for the soffits.

The design followed the basic requirements for swift nesting sites. The size and placing of the entrance (28 mm high x 60 mm long) is important, as a box must permit young swifts adequate space to exercise their wings prior to leaving the nest, while the small height of the entrance excludes starlings and other larger birds. The greater length allows for the swifts' exceptionally long wings.

Placing the entrance at one end and below the space allows maximum space inside the cavity and allows for another speciality of swifts – which is the ability to zoom directly into the nest from below without a pause.

Swifts are colonial nesters, and this design provides four potential nest sites on each of four gable ends. Once installed these elegant nest sites look like a decorative element on the building, and there is no indication that they are bird boxes! How many decorative elements on buildings could be adapted for biodiversity?

Judges' Comments

"Straight to the point, this simple, real world scheme involves the installation of swift nesting boxes on an apartment block. Although this project tackles a single issue and was therefore ineligible for a main award, it was selected for a commendation because it is a practical small-scale demonstration of what can be achieved for species of conservation concern through simple interventions on buildings."

Rehabilitation, North London
Stephen Choi and Sofie Pelsmakers of Architecture for Change,
with Chloe Rayfield and Cristina Blanco
IHDC 2011 Finalist

Project Overview

This proposal centres on the existing built stock, and how individual or large scale 'rehabilitation' can not only decrease energy use and fuel bills, but can also support biodiversity at different scales – from the single garden up to the wider neighbourhood. Careful choice and application of vegetation to attract native species, while also coping with a changing climate, can in turn create a more desirable environment for both humans and native wildlife to thrive while simultaneously contributing to climate change mitigation and adaptation.

The project is a series of adaptive measures that could take us from where we are now – an environment of greyness with sporadic and minimal biodiversity integration – through to a fundamentally different way of understanding the benefits of ecosystems thinking and ecosystems services.

The proposal takes two scenarios – firstly, what could be done today in the current, rather austere climate? It sets out a series of "bottom-up" approaches to integrating biodiversity and improving one's home, using a budget of £10,000 as offered in the Green Deal. Small measures such as reducing impermeable surfaces together with increasing the diversity and number of potential habitats go towards rehabilitating the otherwise rather sterile environment.

The second set of proposals builds on the "austerity measures", introducing "green sky thinking". Birds, bats, invertebrates and amphibians thrive within the gardens, streets and fabric of buildings brought up to Passivhaus standards, driven by a more engaged and educated public sector.

Judges' Comments

"This project tackles the important issue of how we retrofit our existing housing stock to provide ecosystem services and benefit biodiversity. It envisages how terraced homes would be given a green makeover, with features including external cladding, green roofs, climbers, street trees and bird and bat boxes."

Rehabilitation

The Existing...

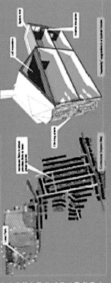
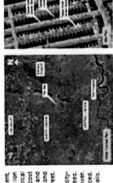
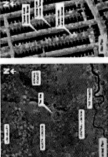
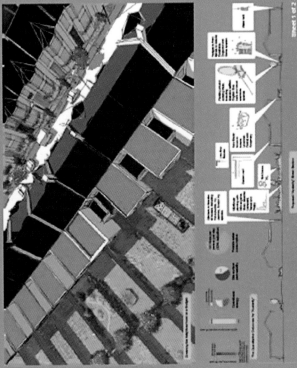
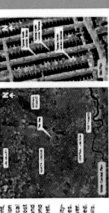

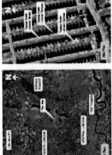
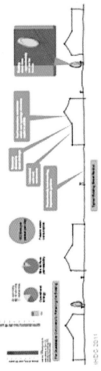

Prototype

An "Austerity" Package...

Rehabilitation Prototype
A "Green-Sky-Thinking" Package...

AfC
ARCHITECTURE FOR CHANGE

Summary of the proposal

The proposal centres on the existing built stock, and how an individual or large scale 'rehabilitation' can not only decrease energy use and fuel bills, but can also support biodiversity at different scales – from the single garden up to the wider neighbourhood. Careful choice and application of vegetation to attract native species, while also coping with a changing climate, can in turn create a more desirable environment for both humans and native wildlife to thrive while simultaneously contributing to climate change mitigation and adaptation. The site location to demonstrate this prototype is a North London neighbourhood.

The project is a series of adaptive measures that could take us from where we are now – an environment of greyness with sporadic and minimal biodiversity integration through to a fundamentally different way of understanding the benefits of ecosystems thinking and ecosystems services. The proposal is described in two parts – firstly, what could be done today in the current, rather austere climate. It sets out a series of "bottom-up" approaches to integrating biodiversity and improving one's home, using a budget of £10,000 as offered in the Green Deal. Small measures such as reducing impermeable surfaces together with increasing the diversity and number of potential habitats go towards rehabilitating our otherwise hostile environment. The second set of proposals builds on the "austerity measures", introducing "green sky thinking". Birds, bats, invertebrates and amphibians thrive within the gardens, streets and fabric of buildings brought up to Passivhaus standards, driven by a more engaged and educated public sector

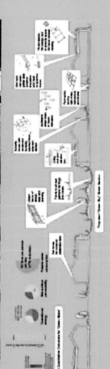

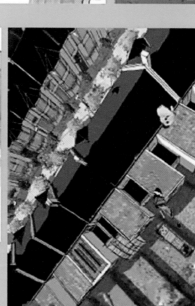

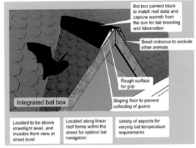

Bat box painted black to match roof slate and capture warmth from the sun for bat breeding and hibernation

Small entrance to exclude other animals

Rough surface for grip

Sloping floor to prevent collecting of guano

Integrated bat box

Located to be above streetlight level, and invisible from view at street level

Located along linear roof forms within the street for optimal bat navigation

Variety of aspects for varying bat temperature requirements

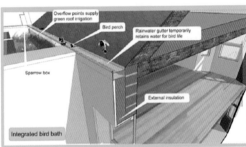

Overflow points supply green roof irrigation

Bird perch

Rainwater gutter temporarily retains water for bird life

Sparrow box

External insulation

Integrated bird bath

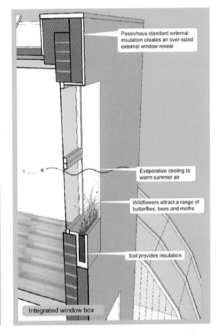

Passivhaus standard external insulation creates an over-sized external window reveal

Evaporative cooling to warm summer air

Wildflowers attract a range of butterflies, bees and moths

Soil provides insulation

Integrated window box

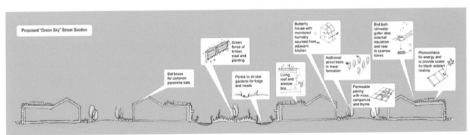

Proposed "Green Sky" Street Section

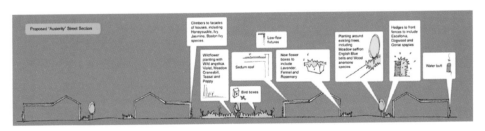

Proposed "Austerity" Street Section

**Neepsend, Sheffield Radu CostinSava
and Xiao Guo, the University of Sheffield BEAU
Research Centre
IHDC 2011 Finalist**

Project Overview

Neepsend Project aims to regenerate the Neepsend Area through a biodiverse approach to landscape and architectural design. The project converts an area located 1.5 km north east of Sheffield City Centre, with a long history of industrial use, into a natural environment rich in biodiversity.

Neepsend Project provides a vital refuge for urban bird species that are threatened by habitat loss, by extending the green area towards sports facilities and key buildings. This concept gives back to nature its lost space, previously occupied by an intensely industrialised area.

The Neepsend Project is also providing low qualified job opportunities in the agricultural sector thus enhancing the surrounding community's life standard.

The UK Biodiversity Action Plan guided the provision of vital refuges for urban bird species threatened by habitat loss, by extending the green area towards sports facilities and other buildings.

This project recreates a natural landform through buildings with a large footprint area. Incorporating exterior and interior inter-connected spaces, natural ventilation systems and a landscape design rich in vegetation, the construction is similar to a large-scale ant hill, and involves retail, accommodation and cultural functions for economically regenerating an economically disadvantaged area.

Judges' Comments

"This proposal for an interesting cluster of lakeside buildings shows how landscape architecture and architecture can blend in an intriguing way when buildings are vegetated. This scheme envisages that every building would be covered in vegetation in order to create a new precinct, where the boundary between buildings and landscape becomes blurred and where drainage, wildlife habitat and microclimate would be improved."

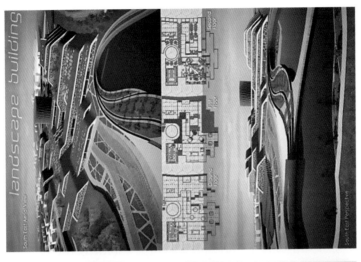

Hebden Bridge Primary School, North Yorkshire
Ryan Groves and Chris Turner
IHDC 2011 Finalist

Project Overview

The design for Hebden Bridge Primary School creates an interactive learning environment that aims to make manifest biodiversity and sustainability.

The pond, orchard and allotments work together to create a mini ecosystem where wildlife can flourish, with bats being the main conservation aim. To attract a wider variety of species of bat, such as the crevice dwelling Pipistrelle, bat box inlets have been designed into some of the building's facades.

The building envelope is designed to Passivhaus standard, resulting in little need for space heating, considerably reducing the building's energy consumption. Apertures are carefully located for spaces to be daylit, with shading devices and overhangs to minimise unwanted solar gain.

A ground source heat pump and photovoltaic panels provide for residual energy needs. Rainwater harvesting is combined with a reverse osmosis water filtration process, filtering rain and waste water to be re-used in the building and in the pond.

Judges' Comments

"This proposal for a new primary school on a sloping site is an attractive, well-mannered scheme. Green roofs are combined with photovoltaic solar panels and bat boxes are provided. Raised vegetable beds would give the pupils hands-on gardening experience. The judges felt that this scheme would need more attention to the functional integration of the various elements in order to be a top prize-winner."

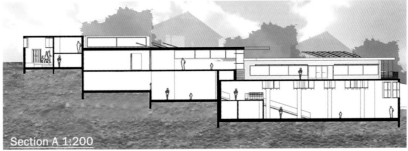

Section A 1:200

II: useful resources

Presented in the order that the issue is encountered in the text

United Nations Department of Economic Affairs – Population Division

This UN organisation monitors, identifies, analyses and investigates policy issues and global trends in the field of population and development. Authoritative source of information on human populations and demographic trends.
http://www.un.org/esa/population/unpop.htm

An Essay on the Principle of Population by Thomas Malthus 1798

Original work by Malthus explaining how population growth outstrips resources. Available online from Project Gutenberg
http://www.gutenberg.org/ebooks/4239

Club of Rome

Think tank responsible for the seminal work Limits to Growth
http://www.clubofrome.org/

Association for the Study of Peak Oil (ASPO)

ASPO is a network of scientists, affiliated with institutions and universities, having an interest in determining the date and impact of the global peak and decline of the world's production of oil and gas, due to resource constraints. ASPO's mission is to:

- Define and evaluate the world's endowment of oil and gas
- Model depletion, taking due account of demand, economics, technology and politics
- Raise awareness of the serious consequences for Mankind

http://www.peakoil.net/

Ecosystem Services Come to Town: Greening Cities by Working with Nature, First Edition. Gary Grant.
© 2012 John Wiley & Sons, Ltd. Published 2012 by John Wiley & Sons, Ltd.

Intergovernmental Panel on Climate Change (IPCC)

The Intergovernmental Panel on Climate Change (IPCC) is the leading international scientific body for the assessment of climate change. It was established by the United Nations Environment Programme (UNEP) and the World Meteorological Organization (WMO) to provide the world with a clear scientific view on the current state of knowledge in climate change and its potential environmental and socio-economic impacts.
http://www.ipcc.ch/

UN Convention on Biological Diversity

Information on the Convention and UN Decade of Biodiversity
http://www.cbd.int/

UN Millennium Ecosystem Assessment

Published in 2005, this huge global study assessed the consequences of ecosystem change for human well-being and the scientific basis for action needed to enhance the conservation and sustainable use of those systems and their contribution to human well-being.
http://www.maweb.org/en/index.aspx

Environmental Literacy Council

This organization provides accurate and free background information on common environmental science concepts. This link features bio-geochemical cycles, but there is plenty of other useful material
http://www.enviroliteracy.org/subcategory.php/198.html

Agroforestry Research Trust

A non-profit making charity which researches into temperate agro-forestry and into all aspects of plant cropping and uses, with a focus on tree, shrub and perennial crops.
http://www.agroforestry.co.uk/

Town and Country Planning Association

With roots that go back to Ebenezer Howard, this think-tank puts social justice and the environment at the heart of the planning policy debate.
http://www.tcpa.org.uk/

Becoming Human

The Institute of Human Origins at the School of Human Evolution and Social Change (SHESC) at Arizona State University conducts, interprets and publicises scientific research on human evolution.
http://www.becominghuman.org/

Volcanic Eruptions

Discover Magazine looks at the most destructive volcanic eruptions in history.
http://discovermagazine.com/photos/23-most-destructive-volcanic-eruptions-in-history

Jared Diamond

Linguist, molecular physiologist, bio-geographer, ornithologist
http://spotlight.ucla.edu/faculty/jared-diamond/

Earth Network

Partnership project looking at pre-industrial European agriculture
http://acl.arts.usyd.edu.au/projects/earth/index.php?option=com_content&task=view&id=12&Itemid=75

The Neolithic of the Levant (1978) by A.M.T. Moore.

PhD thesis which constitutes an excellent account of the prehistoric Near East
http://ancientneareast.tripod.com/NeolithicLevant.html

Greenland Ice Core Project

Findings of the 3 km long ice core drilled from the Greenland Ice Sheet
http://www.ncdc.noaa.gov/paleo/icecore/greenland/summit/document/

Çatalhöyük

Information on the continuing archaeological excavations of the Neolithic settlement at Çatalhöyük, Turkey.
http://www.catalhoyuk.com/

Yangshao Culture

Information on the Neolithic Yangshao Culture which flourished in the Yellow River Valley in China between 5000 and 3000 BC.
http://history.cultural-china.com/en/51History617.html

Mesopotamia 6000-1500 BC

See Room 56 at The British Museum!
http://www.britishmuseum.org/explore/galleries/middle_east/room_56_mesopotamia.aspx

Ancient Egypt

The British Museum's excellent website describing life in Ancient Egypt.
http://www.ancientegypt.co.uk/menu.html

The Indus Civilisation

Huge website describing the little known ancient cities of Harappa and Mohenjo-daro in the Indus Valley
http://www.harappa.com/har/har0.html

The Shang Dynasty

Useful website shows all the dynasties of China – here the Shang Dynasty (1600 – 1046 BC), which was the first Chinese dynasty to leave written records to complement the archaeological evidence, is described.
http://www.hceis.com/chinabasic/history/Shang%20dynasty%20history.htm

Ancient Greece

The British Museum's excellent website describing life in Ancient Greece.
http://www.ancientgreece.co.uk/

Hippodamus

Website describing the work of the world's first town planner, who lived during the fifth century BC.
http://www.mlahanas.de/Greeks/CityPlan.htm

Ancient Rome

The Roman Empire was so large that five departments of the British Museum hold art and artefacts from it. Explore this material through this website.
http://www.britishmuseum.org/explore/cultures/europe/ancient_rome.aspx

Moche

The Moche culture (ca. AD 100-750) was a society with cities, temples, canals and farmsteads located along the arid coast in a narrow strip between the Pacific Ocean and the Andes mountains of Peru.
http://www.latinamericanstudies.org/moche.htm

Foundation for the Advancement of Mesoamerican Studies

Fascinating account of ancient cultures which occurred in Mesoamerica for three thousand years before European contact in the sixteenth century.
http://www.famsi.org/

Florence

Enjoy 360 degree views of Renaissance squares (and links to other Italian cities)
http://www.italyguides.it/us/florence/florence_italy.htm

Bastides

Guide to the medieval planned towns of France
http://about-france.com/tourism/bastide-towns.htm

Versailles

The official website of the Palace of Versailles, created by Louis XIV in the seventeenth century.
http://www.chateauversailles.fr/homepage

Staple Inn

History of Staple Inn, High Holborn, provided by the Institute of Actuaries.
http://www.actuaries.org.uk/research-and-resources/pages/history-staple-inn

Christopher Wren

Buildings designed by Sir Christopher Wren and a short biography of the astronomer and architect.
http://www.greatbuildings.com/architects/Sir_Christopher_Wren.html

Robert Hooke

Biography of Robert Hooke, pioneering seventeenth century scientist.
http://www.ucmp.berkeley.edu/history/hooke.html

London After the Great Fire

The BBC takes a look at how London was transformed after the Great Fire of 1666
http://www.bbc.co.uk/history/british/civil_war_revolution/after_fire_01.shtml

Age of Enlightenment

To understand the natural world and humankind's place in it on the basis of reason and without turning to religious belief was the goal of the seventeenth and eighteenth century intellectual movement called the Enlightenment.
http://history-world.org/age_of_enlightenment.htm

Industrial Revolution

An overview of the Industrial Revolution by Yale University.
http://www.yale.edu/ynhti/curriculum/units/1981/2/81.02.06.x.html
Brindley

Exploring 20th Century London

Here this excellent website takes at look at the Metropolitan Railway – the world's first underground mass transit system
http://www.20thcenturylondon.org.uk/server.php?show=ConInformationRecord.346

Miasma Theory

The Science Museum takes a look at the Miasma Theory of disease, replaced by the Germ Theory in the second half of the nineteeth century
http://www.sciencemuseum.org.uk/broughttolife/techniques/miasmatheory.aspx

Frederick Law Olmstead

A celebration of the life of America's first landscape architect.
http://www.fredericklawolmsted.com/

History of Building Regulations in the British Isles

How fire and other hazards drove people to create building regulations.
http://www.buildinghistory.org/regulations.shtml

Haussmann

How Paris was transformed from a Medieval city to a modern capital between 1858 and 1870
http://gallery.sjsu.edu/paris/architecture/haussman.html

American Planning Association

The APA explains how the basic foundation for planning and zoning in the US was laid by two standard state enabling acts published by the Department of Commerce in the 1920s.
http://www.planning.org/growingsmart/enablingacts.htmZoning

First Garden City Heritage Museum

From Letchworth, the first garden city, information on Ebenezer Howard founder of the Garden City movement.
http://www.gardencitymuseum.org/about_us/history_letchworth_gc/history/ebenezer_howard_founder_letchworth_garden_city

Lewis Mumford Center

The Lewis Mumford Center on Lewis Mumford, the urban planner.
http://mumford.albany.edu/mumford/About_LewisMumford.htm

Royal Parks

Website of London's Royal Parks. This link provides the history of Hyde Park.
http://www.royalparks.org.uk/parks/hyde_park/history.cfm

Central Park

The official website for New York City's Central Park.
http://www.centralparknyc.org/

Island Biogeography

The theory of island biogeography explained by Paul R. Ehrlich, David S. Dobkin, and Darryl Whey.
http://www.stanford.edu/group/stanfordbirds/text/essays/Island_Biogeography.html

International Soil Reference and Information Centre

The World Data Centre for Soils, the World Soil Museum and World Soil Library.
http://www.isric.org/

USGS on the Water Cycle

The United States Geological Survey explains the Water Cycle.
http://ga.water.usgs.gov/edu/watercycle.html

Sewers

This fascinating site looks at the 5,500 year old history of sewers
http://www.sewerhistory.org/

Water

The Natural Resource Defense Council looks at Water
http://www.nrdc.org/water/default.asp

Urban Heat Islands

The US Environmental Protection Agency on the causes, effects and mitigation strategies for this problem
http://www.epa.gov/hiri/

Air Pollution

The World health Organisation's website on air pollution
http://www.who.int/topics/air_pollution/en/

Noise

The US Environmental Protection Agency on the problem of noise
http://www.epa.gov/air/noise.html

Light Pollution

The International dark Sky Organisation campaigns to 'preserve the night'
http://www.darksky.org/

Bird Strike on Buildings

Ontario Nature explains why birds fly into buildings and what can be done to reduce the occurrence of this problem
http://www.ontarionature.org/protect/campaigns/birds_and_buildings.php

Agricultural Land Take

This McGill University website on the history of global land use changes includes an interesting animation
http://www.geog.mcgill.ca/~nramankutty/animation/animation.html

Concrete and Cement

Environmental Building News looks at the environmental impacts of using cement and concrete
http://www.buildinggreen.com/auth/article.cfm/1993/3/1/Cement-and-Concrete-Environmental-Considerations/

Steel

All you need to know about steel construction – here are details of the carbon footprint of steel manufacture and fabrication
http://www.steelconstruction.org/resources/sustainability/carbon-footprints-structures.html

Glass

Treehugger looks at the environmental impacts of glass manufacture
http://www.treehugger.com/culture/ecotip-glass-whats-the-environmental-impact.html

Timber

Here the Totnes Transition Town Project's Energy Descent Action Plan (which is interesting in itself) compares the embodied energy of timber with various other construction materials
http://totnesedap.org.uk/book/appendices/appendix-c/embodied-energy-in-building-materials/

Urban Solid Waste

The World Bank's take on urban solid waste and what can be done
http://web.worldbank.org/WBSITE/EXTERNAL/TOPICS/EXTURBANDEVELOPMENT/EXTUSWM/0,,menuPK:463847~pagePK:149018~piPK:149093~theSitePK:463841,00.html

Peak Phosphorus

Oil is not the only non-renewable resource. This article looks at the issue of phosphorous – a nutrient essential for agriculture.
http://www.energybulletin.net/node/33164

Resilience

Can we cope with climate change and continue to develop in a sustainable way? The Stockholm Resilience Centre is looking for the answers.
http://www.stockholmresilience.org/aboutus.4.aeea46911a3127427980003326.html

Darwin

The London Natural History Museum provides this introduction to the great 19th century naturalist, Charles Darwin
http://www.nhm.ac.uk/nature-online/science-of-natural-history/biographies/charles-darwin/index.html

Linnaeus

Carl Linnaeus, the pioneer of a scientific method of classification of plants
http://www.nhm.ac.uk/research-curation/research/projects/linnaeus-link/

Reductionism and Holism

Willy Østreng of the Norwegian Academy of Science on this fascinating issue
http://www.cas.uio.no/Publications/Seminar/Consilience_Ostreng.pdf

Born-free Foundation

Working to keep wildlife in the wild
http://www.bornfree.org.uk/

Great Lakes

The US EPA provides this key source of information on the Great Lakes
http://www.epa.gov/glnpo/

UN Convention on Biological Diversity

Official website
http://www.cbd.int/history/

Millennium Ecosystem Assessment

The work of more than 1,360 experts making a scientific appraisal of the condition and trends in the world's ecosystems and the services they provide
http://www.maweb.org/en/index.aspx

Atlas of the Biosphere

A wealth of information on ecosystems and human impacts on them
http://www.sage.wisc.edu/atlas/

Cod Fishery

The Canadian Broadcasting Company looks at the collapse of then cod fishery
http://archives.cbc.ca/economy_business/natural_resources/topics/1595/

Urban Wildlife

Learn all about urban nature conservation from the Birmingham and Black Country Wildlife Trust
http://www.bbcwildlife.org.uk/

Green Infrastructure

An American view of green infrastructure:
http://www.greeninfrastructure.net/content/definition-green-infrastructure
And Natural England's advice on the same topic:
http://www.naturalengland.org.uk/ourwork/planningtransportlocal-gov/greeninfrastructure/default.aspx
Sustainable Sites Initiative:
An interdisciplinary effort by the American Society of Landscape Architects, the Lady Bird Johnson Wildflower Center at The University of Texas at Austin and the United States Botanic Garden to create guidelines for sustainable land design, construction and maintenance
http://www.sustainablesites.org/

Town and Country Planning Association

Founded by Sir Ebenezer Howard in 1899 to promote the idea of the Garden City, the TCPA is Britain's oldest charity concerned with planning, housing and the environment.
http://www.tcpa.org.uk/

Biomimcry

Biomimicry is a discipline that studies and then imitates nature's forms and processes to solve human problems
http://biomimicryinstitute.org/about-us/what-is-biomimicry.html

Octavia Hill

Co-founder of the National Trust
http://octaviahill.org/who-was-octavia-hill.html

Hampstead Heath

All about Hampstead Heath in north London
http://www.hampsteadheath.net/index.html

London Natural History Society

One of many similar societies founded in the mid nineteenth century
http://www.lnhs.org.uk/history.htm

Ian McHarg

Biography of the author of the seminal *Design with Nature*, published in 1969
http://www.csiss.org/classics/content/23

Natural History Museum Wildlife Garden

The garden is a haven for thousands of British plants and animals and demonstrates wildlife conservation in the inner city.
http://www.nhm.ac.uk/visit-us/whats-on/wildlife-garden-whatson/index.html

Camley Street Natural Park

Managed by the London Wildlife Trust, this inner London nature reserve was made from an old coal depot in 1984
http://www.wildlondon.org.uk/Pages/Category.aspx?IDCategory=4fd545f7-a11e-4b85-b143-724a886ffa16

Urban Bushland Western Australia

The Urban Bushland Council is a community organisation working for the recognition and protection of urban bushland in Western Australia, a global biodiversity hotspot
http://www.bushlandperth.org.au/about/about-ubc

Bukit Timah Nature Reserve

A surviving fragment of jungle in Singapore
http://www.nparks.gov.sg/cms/index.php?option=com_visitorsguide&task=naturereserves&id=46&Itemid=75

i-Tree

A state-of-the-art, peer-reviewed software suite from the USDA Forest Service that provides urban forestry analysis and benefits assessment tools
http://www.itreetools.org/

Tree Council

Promoting the planting of trees
http://www.treecouncil.org.uk/

Alliance for Community Trees

Supports grassroots, citizen-based nonprofit organisations dedicated to urban and community tree planting, care, conservation, and education
http://actrees.org/site/index.php

Canvey Wick

Buglife (an organisation devoted to the conservation of all invertebrates) describes a species-rich brownfield site in Essex, England
http://www.buglife.org.uk/conservation/currentprojects/Habitats+Action/Brownfields/Conserving+brownfield+invertebrates+in+the+Thames+gateway/canveyislandrainforest

Emsher Park

A regional park established in former industrial land in Germany
http://en.landschaftspark.de/startseite

Urban Farming

All the latest news on how to grow your own food in the city
http://www.urbanfarmonline.com/

UK Biodiversity Action Plan

Published in 1994, this was the UK Government's response to signing the Convention on Biological Diversity (CBD) at the 1992 Rio Earth Summit
http://www.naturalengland.org.uk/ourwork/conservation/biodiversity/protectandmanage/ukactionplan.aspx

Water Sensitive Urban Design

The City of Melbourne explains the principles and practice of Water Sensitive Urban Design (WSUD)
http://wsud.melbournewater.com.au/

Catchment Management

Scottish Natural Heritage on river catchment management issues
http://www.snh.gov.uk/land-and-sea/managing-freshwater/catchment-management/

Rainwater Harvesting

The International Rainwater Harvesting Alliance lobbies for and advocates rainwater harvesting
http://www.irha-h2o.org/

Grey Water Recycling

Household wastewater from kitchen sinks, dishwashers, bathroom sinks, tubs and showers (greywater) can be cleaned and re-used
http://www.letsgogreen.com/greywater-recycling.html

Sustainable Drainage Systems (SuDS)

The Construction Industry Research and Information Association (CIRIA) provides guidance and training on this approach to the drainage of surface water
http://www.ciria.com/suds/

Low Impact Development

A comprehensive land planning and engineering design approach with a goal of maintaining and enhancing the pre-development hydrologic regime of urban catchments
http://www.lowimpactdevelopment.org/

Rain Garden

A shallow depression planted with native plants designed to intercept run-off from a downpipe or paved area
http://www.raingardennetwork.com/

River Restoration

The River Restoration Centre provides information and advice on all aspects of river restoration and enhancement, and sustainable river management
http://www.therrc.co.uk/

Chongyecheong

Official website for this impressive urban river restoration and park project
http://english.sisul.or.kr/grobal/cheonggye/eng/WebContent/index.html

ANC Waters

Singapore's national water agency on its ambitious plans to transform Singapore into a city of of sparkling rivers with landscaped banks, flowing into the picturesque lakes.
http://www.pub.gov.sg/abcwaters/Pages/default.aspx

Bioregions

Planet Drum explains Peter Berg's bioregion concept
http://www.planetdrum.org/

Biomass as energy

Useful source of information on biomass as a fuel source
http://www.biomassenergycentre.org.uk/portal/page?_pageid=76,15049&_dad=portal&_schema=PORTAL

Ecological Networks

Secretariat of the Convention on Biological Diversity reviews global experience of ecological networks, corridors and buffer zones in this document
http://www.cbd.int/doc/publications/cbd-ts-23.pdf

Community Forests

Each Community Forest is is based on a 30-year vision of landscape-scale improvement involving local authorities and local, regional and national partners including the Forestry Commission and Natural England
http://www.communityforest.org.uk/

Green Belts

Green Belts explained
http://www.naturenet.net/status/greenbelt.htmlW
What would Britain look like without Green Belts?
http://www.bbc.co.uk/news/magazine-14916238

All London Green Grid

Learn all about Greater London's green infrastructure network
http://www.designforlondon.gov.uk/what-we-do/all/all-london-green-grid/

Green-Blue Networks

This page looks at green-blue networks, but this French website is also a useful resource for green infrastructure in general (in English)
http://www.cnrs.fr/cw/dossiers/dosbioville_E/contenu/alternative/alter_etape3_2.html

Regional Plans

There is a growing recognition that the region is the arena in which local governments must work together to resolve social and environmental challenges
http://narc.org/regional-councils-mpos/what-is-a-regional-council.html

Masterplans

The Scottish Government provides this helpful summary of what mater plans are and how they can be made to be more effective
http://www.scotland.gov.uk/Publications/2008/11/10114526/2

Living Streets

All about how pedestrians can regain control of the streets
http://www.livingstreets.org.uk/

Design Your Own Park

Using social scientific theory and methods to measure and improve human welfare in neighborhoods
http://bnp.binghamton.edu/projects/dyop/

Guerrilla Gardening

A web portal for the illicit urban gardener
http://www.guerrillagardening.org/

Allotments

Find out how to grow your own vegetables
http://www.allotment.org.uk/

Stormwater Tree Pits

All about stormwater tree pits- helpful information from the Charles River Watershed Association
http://www.crwa.org/projects/bmpfactsheets/crwa_treepit.pdf

Passivhaus

The Passive House Institute on energy efficient building – beware of imitations!
http://www.passiv.de/07_eng/index_e.html

Green Roofs

Plenty of authoritative information and advice on green roofs here
http://livingroofs.org/

Building Biodiversity

Bat bricks and bug houses
http://www.d4b.org.uk/keyConcepts/birdBricks/index.asp

Biodiversity and Planning

A new versatile online resource aimed at helping users to address biodiversity through the planning system and incorporate features that benefit biodiversity in new development
http://www.biodiversityplanningtoolkit.com/

Hundertwasser

Find out more about this remarkable man and his green buildings
http://www.kunsthauswien.com/en/museum/hundertwasser-architecture

Alliance for Healthy Cities

The Alliance for Healthy Cities is an international network aiming at protecting and enhancing the health of city dwellers
http://www.alliance-healthycities.com/htmls/about/index_about.html

Notes and References

Chapter 1

1. Malthus, 1798. Essay on the Principle of Population. http://www.econlib. org/library/Malthus/malPop.html
2. United Nations Department of Economic and Social Affairs, Population Division, Estimates and projections Section http://esa.un.org/unpd/wpp/ index.htm
3. Club of Rome website http://www.clubofrome.org/eng/home/
4. Club of Rome revisited http://www.abc.net.au/science/slab/rome/ default.htm
5. 25th Anniversary of the 1973 Oil Embargo http://www.eia.doe.gov/ emeu/25opec/anniversary.html
6. International Energy Agency World Energy Outlook http://www.world energyoutlook.org/
7. http://www.businessinsider.com/heres-why-the-days-of-abundant-resources-and-falling-prices-are-over-2011-4
8. Intergovernmental Panel on Climate Change http://www.ipcc.ch/index.htm
9. Edward O. Wilson, 2002. The Future of Life. Aldred A. Knopf. New York.
10. United Nations Convention on Biological Diversity http://www.cbd.int/ history/

Chapter 2

1. Fossil reanalysis pushes back the origin of *Homo sapiens* http://www. scientificamerican.com/article.cfm?id=fossil-reanalysis-pushes
2. Late Pleistocene human bottlenecks http://www.bradshawfoundation.com/ stanley_ambrose.php
3. University of Michigan – Global Change Curriculum http://www.global change.umich.edu/globalchange2/current/lectures/human_pop/human_ pop.html
4. Diamond, J., 1991. The Third Chimpanzee. Hutchinson Radius.
5. Neanderthals http://www.mpg.de/english/illustrationsDocumentation/ multimedia/mpResearch/2010/heft03/Evolutionary_Anthropology_ Neantherthal.pdf
6. Atlas of the Human Journey https://genographic.nationalgeographic. com/genographic/lan/en/atlas.html

Ecosystem Services Come to Town: Greening Cities by Working with Nature,
First Edition. Gary Grant.
© 2012 John Wiley & Sons, Ltd. Published 2012 by John Wiley & Sons, Ltd.

7. Who were the Denisovans? http://www.sciencemag.org/content/333/6046/1084
8. Silos of the past: New find reveals ancient food storage structures http://www.scientificamerican.com/blog/60-second-science/post.cfm?id=silos-of-the-past-new-find-reveals-2009-06-24
9. Çatalhöyük http://www.catalhoyuk.com/
10. http://www.etana.org/abzu/abzu-displayentry.pl?RC=20649
11. Crawford, H., 2001. The British Archaeological Expedition to Kuwait, British School of Archaeology in Iraq Newsletter 7 (May): 6.
12. Liverani, M., 1993. Akkad: The First World Empire
13. Standard of Ur http://www.britishmuseum.org/explore/highlights/highlight_objects/me/t/the_standard_of_ur.aspx
14. Tertius Chandler, Four Thousand Years of Urban Growth: An Historical Census.
15. Shaw, I. (Ed) 2000. The Oxford History of Ancient Egypt. Oxford University Press.
16. The Indus Civilisation http://www.harappa.com/har/indus-saraswati.html
17. Yin Xu http://whc.unesco.org/en/list/1114
18. Signe I. and Skydsgaard, J.E., 1995. Ancient Greek Agriculture: An Introduction. Routledge.
19. Aristotle. 350BC. Politics http://classics.mit.edu/Aristotle/politics.2.two.html
20. http://www.bihar.ws/info/History-of-Patliputra--Patna/Pre-Asokan-Magadha-and-what-Magasthanes-had-to-say-about-ancient-Patliputra.html
21. Persian Roads http://www.livius.org/ro-rz/royal_road/royal_road.htm
22. Law of the Twelve Tables http://en.wikipedia.org/wiki/Twelve_Tables
23. Keys, D., 1999. Catastrophe: A Quest for the Origins of the Modern World. Ballantine Books, New York.
24. Laws of the Indies 2012. *Encyclopædia Britannica Online.* http://geoanalyzer.britannica.com/ebc/article-9042315
25. The Bastides of Southwest France http://about-france.com/tourism/bastide-towns.htm
26. Chateau de Versailles http://www.chateauversailles.fr/homepage
27. Encyclopaedia of St Petersburg http://www.encspb.ru/en/
28. The Great Plague of 1665–1666 http://www.nationalarchives.gov.uk/education/lesson49.htm
29. Royal Society http://royalsociety.org/
30. Population history of London http://www.oldbaileyonline.org/static/Population-history-of-london.jsp#a1760-1815

Chapter 3

1. Friends of the Bridgewater Canal http://friendsofbridgewatercanal.org.uk/history.php
2. US Census Bureau Population of the 100 Largest Cities and Other Urban Places in the United States: 1790 to 1990. http://www.census.gov/population/www/documentation/twps0027/twps0027.html
3. Grace's Guide: Stockton and Darlington Railway http://www.gracesguide.co.uk/wiki/Stockton_and_Darlington_Railway

4. Wolmar, C., 2007, Fire and Steam: A History of the Railways in Britain. Atlantic Books (London)

5. London Transport Museum http://www.ltmuseum.co.uk/collections/museum-guide/worlds-first-underground

6. Miasma Theory http://www.sciencemuseum.org.uk/broughttolife/techniques/miasmatheory.aspx

7. John Claudius Loudon http://www.parksandgardens.ac.uk/274/explore-31/historical-profiles-176/john-claudius-loudon-father-of-the-english-garden-477.html?limit=1&limitstart=6

8. Central Park, New York City http://www.centralparknyc.org/about/

9. Ignaz Semmelweis http://www.sciencemuseum.org.uk/broughttolife/people/ignazsemmelweis.aspx

10. John Snow page at UCLA http://www.ph.ucla.edu/epi/snow.html

11. Public health Act 1875 http://www.legislation.gov.uk/ukpga/Vict/38-39/55/contents

12. David H. Pinkney, 1958. Napoleon III and the Rebuilding of Paris. Princeton University Press.

13. http://encyclopedia.chicagohistory.org/pages/323.html

14. City Planning Enabling Act 1928 http://www.archive.org/details/standardcityplan025514mbp

15. New York City Department of Planning: About Zoning http://www.nyc.gov/html/dcp/html/zone/zonehis.shtml

16. Town and Country Planning Association http://www.tcpa.org.uk/

17. Howard, E. (Reprint 1902). Garden Cities of To-Morrow. Faber and Faber. London Available from http://www.library.cornell.edu/Reps/DOCS/howard.htm

18. The Centenary of Hellerau, Garden City http://www.goethe.de/kue/arc/aug/en3561466.htm

19. Letchworth Garden City http://www.letchworth.com/

20. http://www.planninghelp.org.uk/planning-system/history-of-planning-system/town-planning-in-1900s

21. Bagwell. P., 1979. The Transport Revolution 1770–1985. Routledge, London.

22. Litman, T., 2011. Changing Trends and their Implications for Transport Planning, Victoria Transport Policy Institute http://www.vtpi.org/future.pdf

23. Lewis Mumford http://www.albany.edu/mumford/About_us/who_is_lm.html

24. Lewis Mumford, 1938. The Culture of Cities.

25. Sunnyside Gardens http://www.sunnysidegardens.us/history/gardenkids.html

26. Radburn http://www.radburn.org

27. Le Corbusier http://www.open2.net/modernity/4_1.htm

28. Frank Lloyd Wright, Disappearing City (1932)

29. National Parks Service on Atlanta http://www.nps.gov/nr/travel/atlanta/growth.htm

30. Abercrombie Plan http://www.gardenvisit.com/landscape_architecture/london_landscape_architecture/landscape_planning_pos_public_open_space/1943-44_abercrombie_plan

31. Burgess Park, London Borough of Southwark http://www.southwark.gov.uk/info/200280/burgess_park_transformation/1837/design_for_burgess_park

Chapter 4

1. MacArthur R.H. and Wilson, E.O., 1967. The Theory of Island Biogeography. Princeton University Press.

2. Royal Geographical Society http://www.rgs.org/NR/rdonlyres/D0144778-9CFF-4300-A48F-A3BD29FFA782/0/Coralthreats.pdf

3. Wolman, M.G. and Schick, A., 1967. Effects of construction on fluvial sediment, urban and suburban areas of Maryland. Water Resources Research 3:451–464.

4. Anon, 1986. Water Quality on the Tidal Thames. The Environmentalist. Volume 6, Number 4. Springer. Netherlands.

5. Kravčík et al., 2007. Water for the Recovery of the Climate – A New Water Paradigm. http://www.waterparadigm.org/indexen.php?web=./home/homeen.html

6. Karachi Water & Sewerage Board http://www.kwsb.gos.pk/View.aspx?Page=32

7. Pluhowski, E.J., 1970. Urbanization and its effect on the temperature of the streams on London Island, New York. Hydrology and some effects of urbanization on Long Island, New York, Geological Survey professional paper 627-D. United States Government Printing Office. Washington.

8. London Climate Change Partnership http://www.london.gov.uk/lccp/ourclimate/overheating.jsp

9. Lowry W.P., 1998. Urban effects on precipitation amount. Progress in Physical Geography 22, 477–520.

10. National Oceanic and Atmospheric Administration http://www.noaawatch.gov/themes/heat.php

11. UK Climate Impacts Programme http://www.ukcip.org.uk/

12. United Nations Environment Programme (UNEP) Urban Environment Unit http://www.unep.org/urban_environment/issues/urban_air.asp

13. South Coast Air Quality Management District http://www.aqmd.gov/smog/AirQualityData.html

14. Acoustic Ecology Institute http://www.acousticecology.org/wildland biology.html

15. Noise Control Standards in Portland Oregon http://www.portlandonline.com/auditor/index.cfm?c=28705

16. Van Renterghem T. and Botteldooren, D., Green Roofs for Quietness. Acoustics 2008. Paris. http://www.acoustics.org/press/155th/renterghem.htm

17. American Association for Cancer Research http://cancerres.aacrjournals.org/content/65/23/11174.abstract

18. Bat Conservation Trust on bats and lighting http://www.bats.org.uk/pages/bats_and_lighting.html

19. Audubon Lights Out http://www.lightsout.audubon.org/lightsout_history.php

20. Food and Agriculture Organization of the United Nations – Statistics http://www.fao.org/corp/statistics/en/

21. Food and Agriculture Organization of the United Nations – Water http://www.fao.org/nr/water/aquastat/water_use/index4.stm

22. United Nations Development Programme Human Development Reports http://hdr.undp.org/en/

23. Building Greener – Cement http://www.buildinggreen.com/auth/article.cfm/1993/3/1/Cement-and-Concrete-Environmental-Considerations/

24. Sustainable Steel http://www.sustainable-steel.org/energy.html
25. Glass Technology Services http://www.glass-ts.com/News/PressArchive/PressReleases6.html
26. Forest Stewardship Council http://www.fsc.org/
27. The Green Guide to Specification http://www.bre.co.uk/greenguide/page.jsp?id=2069
28. Waste Watch http://www.wasteonline.org.uk/index.aspx
29. Glass Beach, Fort Bragg http://www.fortbragg.com/content/glass-beach
30. Williams P.T., 2005. Waste Treatment and Disposal. Wiley & Sons.
31. Hong Kong Environmental Protection Department http://www.epd.gov.hk/epd/english/environmentinhk/waste/waste_maincontent.html
32. Waste to Energy in Denmark – The most efficient waste management system in Europe http://viewer.zmags.com/showmag.php?mid=wsdps
33. US EPA on composting http://www.epa.gov/epawaste/conserve/rrr/composting/index.htm
34. Haber-Bosch Process http://www.idsia.ch/~juergen/haberbosch.html
35. UNEP: World failing to halt biodiversity decline http://www.cep.unep.org/news-and-events/ap-group-world-failing-to-halt-biodiversity-decline
36. Scientific American: Overfishing could take seafood off the menu by 2048 http://www.scientificamerican.com/article.cfm?id=overfishing-could-take-se
37. Norman Church, Why our food is so dependent on oil http://www.energybulletin.net/node/5045
38. Intergovernmental Panel on Climate Change http://www.ipcc.ch/
39. Association for the Study of Peak Oil and Gas http://www.peakoil.net/about-peak-oil
40. US Energy Information Association http://tonto.eia.doe.gov/country/index.cfm
41. United Nations Department of Economic and Social Affairs http://www.un.org/esa/population/
42. Hirsch Report on Peaking of World Oil Production http://www.netl.doe.gov/publications/others/pdf/Oil_Peaking_NETL.pdf
43. Natural History Museum on Phosphate Recovery http://www.nhm.ac.uk/research-curation/research/projects/phosphate-recovery/p&k217/steen.htm

Chapter 5

1. Natural History Museum on Charles Darwin http://www.nhm.ac.uk/nature-online/science-of-natural-history/biographies/charles-darwin/
2. The Linnaean Society on Linnaeus http://linnean.org/index.php?id=51
3. Ernst Haeckel http://www.mblwhoilibrary.org/exhibits/haeckel/index.html
4. Odum, E. and Odum H.T., 1953. Fundamentals of Ecology. WB Saunders Company. Philadelphia.
5. Rachel Carson, 1962. Silent Spring. Mariner Books, Boston.
6. Born Free Foundation http://www.bornfree.org.uk
7. International Joint Commission http://www.ijc.org/en/activities/consultations/glwqa/guide_3.php
8. UN Convention on Biological Diversity http://www.cbd.int/
9. UN Millennium Assessment http://www.millenniumassessment.org/en/index.aspx

10. UK National Ecosystem Assessment http://uknea.unep-wcmc.org/Home/tabid/38/Default.aspx
11. Gien, L., 2000. Land and Sea Connection: The East Coast Fishery Closure, Unemployment and Health. Canadian Journal of Public Health 91.2: 121–124.
12. Global Restoration Network http://www.globalrestorationnetwork.org/
13. Wildlife Trust for Birmingham and the Black Country http://www.bbcwildlife.org.uk/
14. Green Infrastructure http://www.greeninfrastructure.net/
15. Edward T. McMahon, 2000. Green Infrastructure. Planning Commissioners Journal, Number 37, Winter 2000.
16. The Conservation Fund http://www.conservationfund.org/
17. The Sustainable Sites Initiative http://www.sustainablesites.org/
18. http://www.tcpa.org.uk/pages/green-infrastructure.html
19. Biomimicry Institute http://www.biomimicryinstitute.org
20. Benyus, J., 1997. Biomimicry: Innovation Inspired by Nature. William Morrow & Company, New York.
21. Eastgate Centre, Zimbabwe. http://www.biomimicryinstitute.org/case-studies/case-studies/termite-inspired-air-conditioning.html

Chapter 6

1. National Trust History http://www.nationaltrust.org.uk/main/w-trust/w-thecharity/w-history_trust.htm
2. Hampstead Heath: The Struggle http://www.hampsteadheath.net/the-struggle.html
3. London Natural History Society http://www.lnhs.org.uk/
4. The Ramblers – Our History http://www.ramblers.org.uk/aboutus/history
5. Max Nicholson – Books http://www.maxnicholson.com/books.htm
6. Ian L. McHarg, 1969. Design with Nature. Natural History Press. New York.
7. Mabey, R., 1973. The Unofficial Countryside. Collins, London.
8. London Natural History Museum wildife Garden http://www.nhm.ac.uk/visit-us/whats-on/wildlife-garden-whatson/index.html
9. Camley Street Natural Park http://www.wildlondon.org.uk/Pages/Category.aspx?IDCategory=4fd545f7-a11e-4b85-b143-724a886ffa16
10. National Wildife Federation: In Your Backyard http://www.nwf.org/In-Your-Backyard.aspx
11. Wild About Gardens http://www.wildaboutgardens.org/index.aspx
12. Biodiversity in Urban Gardens – University of Sheffield http://www.bugs.group.shef.ac.uk/
13. Urban Bushland Council Western Australia http://www.bushlandperth.org.au/about/about-ubc
14. Bukit Timah Nature Reserve http://www.nparks.gov.sg/cms/index.php?option=com_visitorsguide&task=naturereserves&id=46&Itemid=75
15. Bukit Timah Eco Bridge http://iyb2010singapore.blogspot.com/2010/05/bridge-for-biodiversity-eco-link-to.html
16. John Evelyn's Sylva http://www.gutenberg.org/files/20778/20778-h/20778-h.htm
17. i-Tree http://www.itreetools.org/
18. Alliance for Community Trees http://actrees.org/site/index.php

19. The Tree Council http://www.treecouncil.org.uk/
20. Phytoremediation – Using plants to clean up soils http://www.ars.usda.gov/is/AR/archive/jun00/soil0600.htm
21. Canvey Island – Britain's Rainforest http://www.buglife.org.uk/conservation/currentprojects/Habitats+Action/Brownfields/Conserving+brownfield+invertebrates+in+the+Thames+gateway/canveyislandrainforest
22. Emscher Landscape Park http://www.metropoleruhr.de/fileadmin/user_upload/metropoleruhr.de/Bilder/Entdecken_Erleben/Emscher_Landschaftspark/PDFs_2011/visitors_guide_Emscher_Landschaftspark_Info_File.pdf
23. Food Up Front – The urban food growing network http://www.foodupfront.org/ and Scaling Up Urban Agriculture in Oakland, CA http://urbanfood.org/
24. Permaculture – A Beginners Guide http://www.spiralseed.co.uk/permaculture/
25. Transition Town Totnes – Nut Trees Project http://www.transitiontowntotnes.org/nuttrees/home
26. Hantz Farms Detroit http://www.hantzfarmsdetroit.com/
27. UK Biodiversity Action Plan http://jncc.defra.gov.uk/default.aspx?page=5155
28. London Olympic Park Biodiversity Action Plan http://www.london2012.com/documents/oda-publications/bap-final-feb09.pdf
29. Southbank Centre http://www.southbankcentre.co.uk/
30. Visit Bankside http://www.visitbankside.com/
31. Minneapolis Riverfront Development Initiative http://minneapolisriverfrontdevelopmentinitiative.com/

Chapter 7

1. Peak Water http://www.worldwater.org/data20082009/ch01.pdf
2. Lake Baikal http://whc.unesco.org/en/list/754
3. UNEP Global Environmental Outlook 4. 2007 http://www.unep.org/geo/geo4/report/acknowledgements.pdf
4. Global Water Consumption Statistics http://www.waterfootprint.org/?page=files/NationalStatistics
5. Rothausen, S.H.A.S. and Conway D., Greenhouse-gas emissions from energy use in the water sector. Nature Climate Change 1, 210–219 (2011) http://www.nature.com/nclimate/journal/v1/n4/full/nclimate1147.html
6. South West Water Final Business Plan 2010–1015 http://www.southwestwater.co.uk/media/pdf/c/e/Formatted_C8.3_for_Review_IM_excised_AB.pdf
7. Kenway S.J., Priestley A., Cook S., Seo S., Inman M., Gregory A. and Hall M. (2008) Energy use in the provision and consumption of urban water in Australia and New Zealand, Water for a Healthy Country National Research Flagship. CSIRO http://www.csiro.au/files/files/pntk.pdf
8. Water Footprint http://www.waterfootprint.org
9. Aral Sea Foundation http://www.aralsea.org
10. Integrated Catchment Management – A review of literature and practice. 2010. New Zealand Ministry for the Environment. http://icm.landcareresearch.co.nz/knowledgebase/publications/public/MfE%20ICM%20Final%20Report%202010_06_28%20Report.pdf

11. Buffer Strip Design. Iowa State University http://www.extension.iastate.edu/Publications/PM1626b.pdf
12. International Rainwater Harvesting Alliance http://www.irha-h2o.org/
13. Grey Water http://www.greywater.com/
14. Sustainable Urban Drainage CIRIA http://www.ciria.org.uk/suds
15. What is Water Senstive Urban Design? http://waterbydesign.com.au/whatiswsud/
16. WSUD Brochure http://library.melbournewater.com.au/content/wsud/MW_WSUD_Brochure.pdf
17. Portland: A sustainable approach to stormwater management http://www.portlandonline.com/bes/index.cfm?c=34598
18. West Michigan Environmental Action Council information on Rain Gardens http://raingardens.org/
19. Schmidt M. 2009. Rainwater Harvesting for Mitigating Local and Global Warming. Fifth Urban Reserch Symposium. World Bank. http://siteresources.worldbank.org/INTURBANDEVELOPMENT/Resources/336387-1256566800920/6505269-1268260567624/Schmidt.pdf
20. Saw Mill River Daylighting http://www.sawmillrivercoalition.org/whats-happening/daylighting-the-saw-mill-river-in-yonkers/
21. River Restoration Centre. Case Study Sutcliffe Park http://www.therrc.co.uk/case_studies/sutcliffe%20park.pdf
22. Quaggy Waterways Action Group http://www.qwag.org.uk/quaggy/restoration.php
23. Cheonggyecheon Official Website http://english.sisul.or.kr/grobal/cheonggye/eng/WebContent/index.html
24. Kallang River – Bishan Park Singapore http://www.pub.gov.sg/abcwaters/ExploreABCAroundYou/Pages/KallangRiverBishanPark.aspx
25. London Heat Map http://www.londonheatmap.org.uk/Mapping/

Chapter 8

1. Peter Berg and Raymond Dasmann, 1977. Reinhabiting California. The Ecologist Vol. 7, Issue 10.
2. Bioregional Congress http://biocongress.org/
3. New York City Watershed Management http://www.citnet.org/New+York+Citys+watershed+protection+praised+UN+Environment+Programme
4. Hong Kong's Country Parks http://www.afcd.gov.hk/english/country/cou_vis/cou_vis.html
5. Water Environment Research Foundation http://www.werf.org/livablecommunities/studies_port_or.htm
6. Norfolk Biodiversity Partnership http://www.norfolkbiodiversity.org/ecologicalnetworks/
7. Greater Norwich Development Partnership http://www.gndp.org.uk/our-work/projects-map/environment/?id=green-infrastructure-delivery-plan
8. Short Rotation Coppice http://www.creff.eu/creff_eng/
9. Citizens' guide to phytoremediation http://www.clu-in.org/download/citizens/citphyto.pdf
10. Nature and Landscape in the Province of North Brabant http://www.ruimtelijkeplannen.nl/web-roo/?planidn=NL.IMRO.9930.sv2010-0003#

11. Ecological Networks in Europe – Country Study for the Netherlands www.ecnc.org/download/normal/…/173/SPEN%20Dutch%20Report.pdf
12. The National Forest http://www.nationalforest.org/forest/
13. UK Government Greenbelt Statistics http://www.communities.gov.uk/publications/corporate/statistics/lagreenbelt2009
14. Ottawa's Greenbelt http://www.canadascapital.gc.ca/bins/ncc_web_content_page.asp?cid=16297-16299-9735-9742&lang=1&bhfv=9&bhfx=9,0,124,0&bhmp=1&bhsh=1050&bhsw=1680&bhsp=102164000&bhqs=1
15. East London Green Grid Framework http://legacy.london.gov.uk/mayor/strategies/sds/docs/spg-east-lon-green-grid-08.pdf
16. The Fatwalk http://www.leariverpark.org/node/367
17. Railway Linesides Biodiversity Action Plan http://www.lambeth.gov.uk/nr/rdonlyres/049c41e9-0c21-458e-b1bc-6ecbe58d89c1/0/bapsummaryrailwaylinesides.pdf
18. Thomas Jefferson Planning District. Eco-logical: Integrating Green Infrastructure and Regional Transport Planning http://www.tjpdc.org/pdf/Environment/Ecologic%20Final%20Report.pdf
19. Adaptation to climate change using green and blue infrastructure. A database of case studies. London Borough of Sutton: Adaptation to flooding via local planning policies http://www.grabs-eu.org/membersArea/files/sutton.pdf
20. Stapleton, Denver http://www.stapletondenver.com/

Chapter 9

1. Appleyard, D., Gerson, M.S. and Lintell, M., 1981. Livable Streets, University of California Press, Berkeley.
2. What is Shared Space? http://www.hamilton-baillie.co.uk/_files/_publications/6-1.pdf
3. Gehl, J. 1987. Life Between Buildings: Using Public Space. Van Nostrand Reinhold, New York.
4. Guerilla Gardening http://www.guerrillagardening.org/
5. Binghampton Neighborhood Project http://bnp.binghamton.edu/projects/empowering-neighborhoods-and-restoring-outdoor-play/
6. Nobel Prize in Economic Sciences 2009, Elinor Ostrom http://www.nobelprize.org/nobel_prizes/economics/laureates/2009/ostrom-lecture.html
7. The Phoenix Garden http://www.phoenixgarden.org/
8. Asset Transfer Unit http://atu.org.uk/
9. National Trust provides 1000 allotments http://www.nationaltrust.org.uk/main/w-global/w-news/w-latest_news/w-news-growing_spaces.htm
10. National Gardening Association http://www.garden.org/
11. 14th International Planning History Society Conference, Istanbul 2010. Neha Goel. Squatter Settlements: The Urban Vernacular? http://www.iphs2010.com/abs/ID102.pdf
12. Liberty Lands Park Rain Gardens http://planphilly.com/liberty-lands-park-could-represent-future-water-management
13. Greening Parking Lots http://www.toronto.ca/planning/urbdesign/greening_parking_lots.htm

14. Trees and Clay Soils http://www.wirral.gov.uk/my-services/environment-and-planning/building-control/guidance-and-advice/foundations-trees-and-clay

15. Tree for Cities http://www.treesforcities.org/

16. The Tree Council http://www.treecouncil.org.uk/

17. National Tree Trust http://www.nationaltreetrust.org/

18. National Tree Day http://treeday.planetark.org/

19. International Tree Foundation http://internationaltreefoundation.org/

20. China to spend billions on tree planting projects http://www.china.org.cn/environment/news/2009-03/12/content_17427454.htm

21. Lindsey, P.A. and Bassuk, N. 1991. Specifying Soil Volumes to Meet the Needs of Urban Street Trees and Trees in Containers. Journal of Arboriculture 17.6: 141–148.

22. Breen, P., et al. 2004. Street Trees as Stormwater Treatment Measures. WSUD 2004.

23. Stormwater Tree Trench http://www.phillywatersheds.org/what_were_doing/green_infrastructure/tools/stormwater_tree_trench

24. Green roofs at the Museum of London http://www.treehugger.com/files/2011/08/green-roof-evolving.php

25. Passive House http://www.passivehouse.com/07_eng/index_e.html

26. Use Water Wisely http://www.wateruseitwisely.com/

27. Energy Saving Trust http://www.energysavingtrust.org.uk/

28. The UK Rainwater Harvesting Association http://www.ukrha.org/

29. About greywater reuse http://greywateraction.org/content/about-greywater-reuse

30. Moos Water Filtration Plant, Wollishofen, Zurich http://www.greenroofs.com/projects/pview.php?id=680

31. Gaffin, S., Parshall, L., Beattie, D., Berghage, R., O'Keeffe, G. and Braman, D. 2005. Energy Balance Modelling Applied to a Comparsion of White and Green Roof Cooling Efficiency. 3rd Annual Green Roof and Wall Conference Washington DC.

32. Sandifer, S. and Givoni, B. 2002. Thermal Effects of Vines on Wall Temperatures – Comparing Laboratory and Field Collected Data. SOLAR 2002, Proceedings of the Annual Conference of the American Solar Energy Society. Reno.

33. Miller et al. 2004. Case Study: Vegetation on building facades: 'Bioshader'. Centre for Sustainability of the Built Environment/University of Brighton/University of Rouen.

34. Ivy and buildings http://www.geog.ox.ac.uk/research/landscape/rubble/ivy/

35. City of Chicago http://egov.cityofchicago.org/city/webportal/portalDeptCategoryAction.do?deptCategoryOID=−536889314&contentType=COC_EDITOR

36. Liu, K.Y. and Baskaran A. 2005. National Research Council of Canada. http://www.nrc-cnrc.gc.ca/eng/ibp/irc/ctus/ctus-n65.html

37. Onmura S., Matsumoto, M. and Hokoi, S. Study on evaporative cooling effect of roof lawn gardens. Energy and Buildings 2001;33:653–66.

38. Kumar, R., Kaushik, S.C. 2005. Performance evaluation of green roof and shading for thermal protection of buildings. Building and Environment Volume 40 Pages 1505–1511.

39. Schmidt, M. 2007. Presentation to International Water Conference, Berlin. http://www.iwc-berlin.de/medienpool/iwc_m77_61000000012/iwc_20071011142009_1_840856.pdf

40. Green roofs and storm water runoff http://livingroofs.org/2010030671/green-roof-benefits/waterrunoff.html

41. German Landscape Society (FLL) Guidance on Green Roofs http://www.fll.de/shop/product_info.php?info=p152_Green-Roofing-Guideline--2008--download-edition-.html

42. Nagase, A. et al. 2010. An evaluation of biotope green roof in Japan. Proceedings of the World Green Roof Congress London.

43. Brenneisen, S., 2002. Vogel, Kafer und Spinnen auf Dachbegrunungen – Nutzungsmoglichkeiten und Einrichtungsoptemeierungen. Geographisches Institut Basel Universitat Basel/Baudepartment des Kantons Basel-Stadt.

44. An Introduction to LEED http://www.usgbc.org/DisplayPage.aspx?CategoryID=19

45. BREEAM http://www.breeam.org/

46. Vancouver Convention Centre http://www.vancouverconventioncentre.com/thefacilities/environment/

47. World Expo 2010 http://en.expo2010.cn/

48. Singapore's Skyrise Greenery http://www.skyrisegreenery.com/

49. House sparrow http://www.rspb.org.uk/ourwork/projects/details.aspx?id=tcm:9–235650

50. Bird nest box designs: http://www.the-scoop-on-wild-birds-and-feeders.com/baby-birds.html http://extension.oregonstate.edu/catalog/pdf/ec/ec1556.pdf http://www.rspb.org.uk/advice/helpingbirds/nestboxes/smallbirds/index.aspx http://www.perthzoo.wa.gov.au/Animals–Plants/Fauna-friendly-Gardens/Nest-Boxes-for-Native-Animals/

51. Schwegeler bird and bat boxes http://www.schwegler-natur.de/

52. Bat Conservation Trust on bat boxes http://www.bats.org.uk/publications_detail.php/234/bat_boxes_your_questions_answered

53. UK Green Building Council http://www.ukgbc.org/about-us

54. Lapwings nesting on green roofs http://dustygedge.co.uk/roadblog/2010/06/lapwing-green-roof-central-switzerland/comment-page-1/

55. Richardson, Benjamin W. 1876. Hygeia – A City of Health. MacMillan. London http://www.gutenberg.org/ebooks/12036

56. Article on rooftop farming in Washington Post http://www.washingtonpost.com/wp-dyn/content/article/2009/09/11/AR2009091103836.html

57. Rooftop agriculture in Florida by Kevin Songer http://www.kevinsonger.blogspot.com/

Index

Abercrombie 36, 37, 103
Abstraction 82, 86, 97
Accounts 11
Acid rain 45
ACROS Building 133
Adamson (Bo) 123
Adamson (Joy) 56
Adaptation 52, 60, 101, 116
Adobe 17
Adornment 3, 11
Africa 8, 10, 16, 82, 120
Agriculture 1, 6, 7, 14–24, 48, 50, 56,
    76–7, 82, 137
Agro-forestry 77
Aircraft 47
Airport 37, 46, 107
Air quality 46, 49, 53, 59, 91, 105, 120
Akkad 17–19
Albedo 125
Alexandria 15, 16
Alliance for Community Trees 73
All London Green Grid 103, 104
Allotments 36, 115
Ambasz (Emilio) 133
American Revolution 23
Ammonia 50, 51
Amphibians 77, 103
Amphitheatre 16
Amsterdam Bos 68
Anatolia 9, 12, 14, 15
Ancient Rome 1, 16
Andes 17
Anyang 14
Apollo 57
Appleyard (Donald) 112
Appliances 37, 48, 123
Aquatic wildlife 42

Aquifers 43, 82, 83, 85, 93, 123
Arable 9
Aral Sea 83
Archaeological 8
Aridity 11
Aristotle 15
Arithmetic 11
Army 12
Army Corp of Engineers 90
Art 11
Artillery 19
Ashoka 15
ASLA 61
Asphalt 32, 44, 88, 113, 125
Asset transfer 115
Astronomy 11
Atlanta 11
Atlantic 16, 59
Attenuation 88, 129
Augustus 16
Australia 71, 83, 86, 101, 118, 120, 134
Austria 116, 118, 139
Avenue 17, 20, 28, 120
Aztec 19

Baghdad 16
Baikal 81
Bangkok 29
Banking 20
Banksia 71
Barbican 122
Barbon (Nicholas) 20
Barley 9, 10, 12
Barlow Commission 35
Basel 126, 131–3
Basildon 35
Bastides 19, 114

Ecosystem Services Come to Town: Greening Cities by Working with Nature,
First Edition. Gary Grant.
© 2012 John Wiley & Sons, Ltd. Published 2012 by John Wiley & Sons, Ltd.

Bat 47, 130, 134, 135
Baumann (Natalie) 135
Beef 48,
Bees 74, 128
Beijing 81
Belgium 116
Benz (Karl) 31
Benzene 46
Berg (Peter) 95
Berlin Wall 89
Bicycle 23, 53
Binghampton 113
Biodiversity 4, 5, 33, 37, 40, 49, 51, 53, 55, 59,
    60, 66, 67, 70, 71, 74, 77, 86, 114, 117–19,
    130–134, 137, 138, 140
Biodiversity Action Plans 77
Bioengineering 92
Bio-geochemical cycles 5
Biomass (Energy) 99, 100, 103
Biomes 95
Biomimicry 62,
Bioregions 95, 96, 99, 134
Biosphere 59
Birds 1, 47, 56, 66, 67, 77, 105, 114, 130,
    134, 135
Birkenhead Park 26
Birmingham 24, 45
Bishan Park 92
Bitumen 32
Black Country 45, 99, 100, 106
Black Death 19
Black redstart 131, 132
Blanc (Patrick) 127
Blue Marble 57
Blue networks 105
Bosch (Carl) 50,
Boston 36
Bottleneck 8
Boulevard 28
Brazil 37, 134
Breast cancer 47
BREEAM 133
Brenneisen (Stephan) 131
Bridge (green) 72, 101
Bridgewater Canal 23
Brindley 23
Britain 23, 24, 26, 31, 68, 69, 79, 82
Broadacre 33
Bronze Age 12

Brooklyn 136
Brownfield 74, 75, 131, 132
Brown roofs 132
Buckland 66
Buddhism 16
Buddliea 103
Buenos Aires 91
Buglife 74
Building standards 27, 37
Bukit Timah 71
Burgess Park 36
Burnham (Daniel) 29
Burton-on-Trent 101
Buses 31, 46
Butterflies 41, 69, 75, 86, 133

California 50,
California Academy of Sciences 132
Camden Town 24, 25
Camley Street 69,
Canal 14, 15, 17, 23, 24, 56
Canoes 8
Canvey Wick 74, 75
Carbon 49, 52, 76, 82, 83, 123, 124, 141
Carbon dioxide 41, 48, 49, 51
Carbon monoxide 46
Cars 31, 34, 73, 85
Carson (Rachel) 56
Caste 12
Çatalhöyük 9,10
Catchment 43, 63, 84, 89–91, 96,
    97, 117, 118
Catskill 96
Cattle 10, 11, 48
Causeways 17
Celestial alignments 17
Cement 48, 135
Cenotes 17
Central Park 26, 27, 41, 67
Ceramics 17
Chamberlain (Neville) 35
Chang'an 16
Channelisation 43
Charcoal 14
Chariots 14
Charlottesville 105
Cheonggyecheon 90, 91
Cheshire 68
Chiao Wei yo 14

Chiba University 130
Chicago 29, 30, 45, 47, 56, 128
Chicanes 112
Chimneys 20, 27
China 10, 13–15, 120, 134
Cholera 26, 28
Chowk 116
Cisterns 10, 118
Citadel 18, 133
Citizens 29, 30, 50, 59, 72, 111, 113–17,
    138, 140
City centre 29, 34, 77, 122
City Hall (Chicago) 128
City-region 99, 105, 107
City-states 12, 33, 91
Civilisation 1–5, 7, 12–14, 17, 18, 51, 63,
    82, 137
Clan 116
Clapham (Arthur) 55
Clapton Park Estate 119
Clay 72, 120
Cleveland 56
Climate change 3, 5, 7, 12, 17, 45, 51,
    52, 60, 63, 82, 84, 86, 93, 101, 103,
    106, 121, 140
Climatologists 45
Closed-loop 63, 137
Club of Rome 3, 57
Coal 2, 23, 24, 49–51
Coalfields 25
Cold War 89
Cole (Lyndis) 68
Colonnades 19
Columbia River 97
Combined heat and power 99
Combined sewers 43, 85
Community forests 101
Commuters 29
Concrete 33, 48, 49, 67, 74, 78, 83, 90,
    92, 125
Conservation Fund 60
Constantinople 16
Convention on Biological Diversity 58
Conveyance 88
Cook County Hall 128
Cool roofs 125
Cooperatives 31
Coral 42
Cordoba 121

Core (eco-network) 41, 60, 71
Core (urban) 44, 122
Courtyards 33, 116
Crop failure 10, 13
Crop rotations 24
Croton 96
Crude oil 3, 32
Cumra 9
Cuttings 24, 34, 103
Cyanide 50
Cycling 30, 99, 105, 113, 136, 138

Daimler-Chrysler 89
Dams 56, 97
Darlington 24,
Darmstadt 123
Darwin 2, 55
Darwinism 66
Dasmann (Ray) 95
Dead Sea 8, 56
Decay 41, 130
Deforestation 1, 56
Delaware (watershed) 96
Delhi 116, 117
Deltas 11
Demolition 24, 27, 37
Den Bosch 100
Denisovans 8
Denmark 116
Denver 107, 108
Department of Energy 52
Desalination 83, 92, 123
Design with Nature 68
Detroit 56, 77
Dialogue 74
Diamond (Jared) 8
Dioxins 46
Disease 19, 20
Distinctiveness 34
Disturbance 41, 71, 135
Ditches 12, 17, 101
Dogs 10
Drainage 27, 32, 37, 42, 82, 85, 86, 88, 89, 95,
    99, 107, 117, 120, 121, 130
Dresden 30
Drought 8, 10, 12, 13, 17, 52, 82, 87, 89, 93,
    120, 131, 137
Drying 42, 43, 82, 83, 93, 123
Dust 42, 44

Earth Summit 58
Eastgate Centre 62, 63
East London Green Grid 103
Ecological corridors 90, 103
Ecological networks 41, 71, 72, 100–102
Ecology 5, 55, 56, 68, 69
Economic growth 3, 35
Eco-roofs 99
Ecosystem approach 58, 59, 61, 63
Ecosystem services 4, 36, 40, 42, 58–62, 63,
    72, 79, 86, 97, 99, 140
Eco-towns 62
Egypt (ancient) 13–16
Eindhoven 100
Electric vehicles 46
Elites 11
Emerald necklace 36
Emmen 135
Emscher Park 75
Encapsulated countryside 70, 71
Endless Village 69
Engineers 33, 37, 42, 62, 77, 88, 90
England 26, 27, 30, 34, 50, 60, 66, 67, 77, 83,
    99, 101, 105, 115, 131
Enlightenment 23, 55, 72, 137
Entertainment 2, 16, 27, 56
Environmental Protection Agency 97
Epiphytes 127
Equitable Building 29
Eridu 12
Erie (Lake) 56
Erosion 14, 41, 42, 59, 130
Euphrates 12
Euston 24
Eutrophic 42
Evaporation 12, 82, 93
Evapo-transpiration 44, 82, 86, 93, 118, 125,
    128, 129
Evelyn (John) 72,
Excavations (archaeological) 8
Extensive green roof 47, 89, 122, 129,
    131–3, 135
Extinction 1, 41, 43

Facades 126
Factories 26, 27, 29, 37, 45, 50
Faeces 26, 44
Families 11, 26, 34, 116
Famine 11, 17, 24

Farming 11, 51, 76, 77, 137, 138
Fatwalk 103
Feist (Wolfgang) 123
Fertiliser 50–52
Festival of Britain 79
Festivals 11, 18
Fields 4, 9, 49, 84
Finance 2
Finland 116
Fire 1, 8, 19, 20, 30, 37, 130
Fire Brigade 16
Flanner (Ben) 136
Flash lock 14
FLL 134
Flood 10, 17, 32, 42, 43, 58–60, 78, 84, 85, 89,
    90, 93, 99, 105–7, 118, 130, 137, 138
Floodplain 9, 11–13, 89, 106, 107
Florida 135, 136
Fluvial 106
Food 2–5, 14, 18, 21, 26, 41, 46–8, 51, 53, 58,
    59, 76, 81–3, 95, 103, 107, 116, 138
Foraging 11
Ford 31
Forests 2, 4, 5, 11, 14, 49, 73, 101, 113,
    137, 138
Fort Bragg 50
Fortresses 11
Forum 16
Fossil fuels 2–4, 39, 99
Foul water 37, 43, 85
Fragmentation 24, 41
France 19, 36, 99, 116
Frank Lloyd Wright 33
Freight 37
French Revolution 23
Fukuoka 133
Fundamentalism 23

Galleys 14
Ganges 15
Garden Cities 30, 31, 35
Gardens, 8, 14, 21, 22, 27, 28, 32, 33, 36, 60,
    72, 84–9, 97, 99, 103, 112–14, 117, 118,
    122, 129, 133, 136, 138
Gary (Indiana) 56
Geddes (Patrick) 29
Gedge (Dusty) 131
Gehl (Jan) 112, 113
Geology 84, 85, 88

Georgia 35
Gerard 65
Germ (theory of disease) 28
Germany 27, 30, 50, 75, 89, 99, 116, 118, 123
Glass 21, 49
Glass Beach 50
Goel (Neha) 116
Gold 17
Gonzaga 133
Goodwood 135
Granary 9
Grand Canal 14
Grand Mosque 121
Grantham (Jeremy) 3
Grasses 9
Grassland 8, 70, 74, 77, 89, 113, 131
Grazing 48, 65
Grazing marsh 74
Great Depression 26
Great Lakes 56, 57, 84
Great Leap Forward 8
Great Pyramid 13
Great War 31
Greece 134
Green belt 30, 35, 101, 102, 111, 138
Green-blue veining 101
Green Book 107
Green grids 103
Greenhouse gas 4, 41, 49, 51, 83, 95, 99, 137
Green infrastructure 60–62, 63, 68, 72, 73, 75,
    79, 91, 99, 102, 103, 105–7, 140
Greening 3, 5, 39, 62, 95, 101, 109, 111, 113,
    114, 118, 119, 122, 123, 136
Greenland (ice core) 9
Green roof 47, 77, 85, 86, 88, 89, 99, 105, 122,
    125, 128–36
Green Roof Consultancy 122
Green space 29, 30, 33, 60, 65, 67–9, 77,
    78, 89, 91, 93, 99, 102, 103, 105–7, 115,
    117, 140
Greenways 36, 60
Grey water 85, 92, 123, 124, 128
Grids 13, 15, 17, 19, 107
Ground source heat pumps 123
Growing medium 127–9
Growth 2, 3, 7, 11, 12, 16, 25, 33, 35, 50, 57,
    65, 101
Guano 50
Guerrilla gardeners 113

Haber (Fritz) 50
Haber-Bosch Process 50, 52
Habitat 4, 8, 34, 40, 41, 48, 49, 53, 60,
    69–71, 74, 77, 79, 86, 89, 90, 92,
    99, 101, 105–7, 130–133,
    135, 138
Hackney 118, 119
Hampstead Heath 65, 66, 93
Hancock Center 47
Hantz Farms 77
Harappa 13
Harare 62
Haussmann 28, 29
Hazards 59, 82
Headquarters 27
Health 26, 30, 37, 46, 56, 83, 85, 105, 116,
    136, 138, 140
Heat wave 44, 45, 52
Heavy metals 42, 44, 84, 86
Hellerau 30
Henan 10, 14
Herball 65
Highways 34, 35
Hill (Octavia) 65
Hinterlands 11, 95, 99, 138
Hippodamus 15
Hirsch Report 52
Hominid 8
Homo sapiens 8
Honeydew 73
Hong Kong 33, 50, 97
Hooke 20
Hope 5, 7
Horse 16, 24, 25, 31
Hotspot 70, 71
House martin 134
House sparrow 134
Housing 13, 26, 28, 33, 35, 74, 116, 118
Howard (Ebenezer) 29–31
Huaca de la Luna 17
Hubbert 3
Hummingbirds 133
Hundertwasser 137, 139
Hunter-gatherer 1, 7, 8
Hunting 11, 22, 41
Huron (Lake) 57
Hyde Park (Chicago) 29
Hydrology 33
Hydroponic 127

Ice 9, 11, 52, 82
Ice age 8
Ice dam 11
Ice sheets 8, 11
Illinois 29
Impacts 4, 39, 41, 47, 71, 105, 131
India 13, 116
Indus 12, 13
Industrial Revolution 1, 2, 22–4, 50, 55, 63, 65, 137
Industry 5, 14, 24, 35, 37, 44, 52, 56, 62, 73, 83, 137
Infiltration 88, 118, 122
Informal settlements 37, 116, 117
Infrastructure 4, 16, 26, 27, 33, 37, 40, 41, 60, 62, 63, 97, 116
Innovation 11, 50, 62, 140
Insects 47, 66, 73
Insulation 123
Intensive green roof 129, 133
Intergenerational (equity) 61
International Energy Agency 3
International Tree Foundation 120
Invertebrates 74, 77, 78, 130–132
IPCC 51
Iraq 12
Iron Age 14
Iron ore 26,
Irrigation 11–14, 17, 48, 82, 85, 88, 89, 97, 114, 118, 123, 128, 130
Island biogeography 41
Italy 2, 19, 133
Ivy 126

Japan 29, 35, 36, 50, 130, 133
Jermy (Clive) 69
Jewellery, 13
Jiangsu 14, 15
Jones (Richard) 132
Jordan 8, 9
Journal of Public Health 136
Jubilee Walkway 79

Kadas (Gyongyver) 132
Kallang River 92
Kansas 48
Karachi 43
Kenya 37
Kephart (Paul) 133

Kerbs 87, 112
Khichripur 116
Khufu 13
Kinder Scout 67
King's Cross 25
Konya 9
Krakatoa 17

Ladder 9
Lamprey 56
Laurentian (Ice Sheet) 11
Lead (metal) 46
Lebanon 14
Le Corbusier 33
LEED 132
Lee Myung-bak 91
Lee Valley Regional Park 103
Legislation 19, 26, 31, 32, 35, 46, 50
Leicester 101
Letchworth 30, 31
Liberty Lands Park 118
Lighting 47, 53, 113, 120
Light pollution 47
Lima 81
Limestone 48
Limits to Growth 3, 57
Linnaeus 55
Litman 31
Litter 42, 44, 131
Little (John) 119
Liveability 3
Liverpool 24
Living streets 112, 113
Living walls 46, 85, 122, 126–8, 134
Locks 24
Locomotives 24
London 16, 19–22, 24–6, 30, 31, 35–7, 41, 43, 44, 65–7, 69, 70, 72, 73, 77–9, 90, 93, 101, 103, 104, 107, 114, 115, 118–20, 122, 128, 131, 132, 134, 139
London Building Act 27
London County Council 65
London Heat Map 93
London Natural History Society 66
Long Island 35, 44
Los Angeles 32, 35, 48
Loudon (John Claudius) 26
Loxton (Mark) 69

Lucca 18, 19
Luxembourg 116
Luzern 135

Mabey (Richard) 68, 74
MacArthur 41
Macedon 14
Malthus 2
Manchester 23, 24, 105
Manpower 11
Mantua 133
Manure 21, 31, 50, 53
Marketplaces 11
Marshes 26
Masonry 13, 16, 19–21, 44, 45, 128
Massachusetts 36
Massachusetts Institute of Technology 3
Masterplanning 107, 109
Mayans 17
McHarg 68
McMahon 60
Mega-colossal eruption 8
Melbourne 88, 89
Mercantile capitalism 19
Mesoamerica 17
Mesopotamia 11–13
Metalworkers 11
Methane 46
Metropolises 35
Metropolitan Railway 25
Mexico City 81, 82
Miasma 26, 27, 60, 67
Michigan (Lake) 56
Microbes 85, 88
Microclimate 43, 44, 53, 60, 120, 124, 128, 130, 140
Microscopes 20
Middle East 11
Middle Kingdom 13
Migratory birds 105
Miletus 15
Millennium Ecosystem Assessment 58, 59
Mills 24
Milwaukee 56
Minneapolis Riverfront 79
Mississippi 79
Moche 16, 17
Mohenjo-daro 13
Monsoon 13

Mosaics (habitat) 131
Mosquitoes 84
Mountains 35
Multi-ethnic 17
Multi-functional design 60, 62, 86
Mumford (Lewis) 32, 33
Museum of London 122
Muthesius (Hermann) 30

Nagase (Ayako) 130
Nairobi 37
Nasiriyah 12
National Ecological Network 100
National Ecosystem Assessment 59
National Forest 101
National Parks Board 92
National Tree Trust 120
National Trust 65, 116
National Wildlife Federation 69
Natufian 8
Natural gas 49, 51
Natural History Museum 69, 70
Naturalists 66, 67, 74
Neanderthal 8
Near East 8, 10, 14
Neighbourhoods 24, 35, 111, 113, 119, 140
Neolithic Revolution 9, 10
Nest boxes 134, 135
Netherlands 27, 100, 112, 116, 122
Networks 5, 11, 17, 19, 24, 34, 35, 41, 43, 60, 63, 71, 72, 79, 100–102, 105–7, 109, 138
New Jersey 33
New towns 35, 36, 68
New York City 24, 26, 27, 29, 35, 37, 96, 97
New York State 96, 97
Nicholson (Max) 67–9
Nijmegen 122
Nile 12, 13
Nitrates 44
Nitrogen oxides 45, 49
Noise 37, 46, 47
Noord-Brabant 100
Norfolk 99
Norfolk Wildlife Trust 99
Norway 116
Norwich 99
Nuneaton 50
Nutrient cycling 59

Oceania 8
Odum 55
Office 34, 128
Officials 11, 16, 37
Oil Age 2, 31, 51
Oil Crisis 3, 74
Olmsted 26, 30
Olympic Park 77, 78, 103
Onagers 12
Ontario (Lake) 56
Open Spaces Society 65
Oregon 46, 86, 87, 97, 101, 118, 122
Origins 7, 23, 25
Ostrom 114
Ottawa 101
Oxford Road Corridor 105
Oxford University 126
Ozone 46

Paddington 25
Pakistan 13, 43
Palaces 11, 13, 14, 17, 19
Papua 10
Paris 16, 28, 29, 33
Parker (Barry) 31
Parking 34, 118
Parklands 41
Parks 19, 22, 26, 28, 30, 33, 36, 37, 41, 60,
    67, 69, 74, 77, 78, 89, 92, 97, 101–3,
    111–15, 138
Passivhaus 123
Pastoralists 11
Patagonia 8
Pataliputra 15
Pathogens 10, 84, 124
Patna 15
Paved roads 16, 37
Peak Oil 3, 52
Peak Phosphorus 52
Pearce (Mick) 62
Permaculture 76, 132, 135
Permeable paving 86
Peroxyacetyl nitrate 46
Persian Empire 16
Perth 42, 70, 71
Peru 17
Pests 9, 59, 134
Pharaohs 13
Pharmaceuticals 59

Philadelphia 118, 122
Philippines 19
Phoenix Garden 114, 115
Phosphates 52
Photochemical (smog) 46
Photosynthesis 2, 59, 125
Photovoltaic (cells) 123
Phytoremediation 74, 99
Piazza 20, 122
Piazza del Campo 18
Pipelines 83
Piraeus 15
Planet Ark 120
Planners 28, 37, 60, 99, 105, 116
Planning 5, 19, 26, 29, 31–3, 35, 36, 41, 46,
    58, 60, 61, 68, 74, 77, 86, 105, 107, 109,
    111, 117, 138
Planting 26, 34, 46, 72, 77, 87, 88, 105, 113,
    114, 118–20, 128, 133, 134
Plan Voisin 33
Playing fields 36
Plazas 17
Plot 33, 76, 107, 115, 116
Ploughing 24
Pneumatic tyres 31
Poland 71, 116
Police 16
Politics 2
Pollutants 42, 45, 46, 86, 88, 118, 120
Pollution 1, 3, 4, 27, 37, 44–7, 53, 67, 81, 82,
    89, 97, 120
Ponds 69, 70, 84–6, 88, 89, 130
Population 1–4, 8, 10–13, 16, 19, 22–4, 28, 30,
    33, 41, 48, 50–53, 57, 77, 81, 84, 99, 103,
    105, 131, 136, 137
Portland (Oregon) 46, 86, 87, 97, 118, 122
Potato 10
Potsdamer Platz 84, 89
Potters 11
Pottery 8
Pound lock 14
Power 2, 11, 13, 17, 19, 23, 24, 26, 37, 44, 45,
    50, 51, 53, 99
Precautionary Principle 61
Precipitation 82
Predator-prey 46
Preservation 60, 61, 65, 138
Priests 11
Printing 20

Promenade 78, 79
Provisioning services 58, 59
Public health 37, 46, 136
Public Health Act 26
Public realm 20, 29, 77, 111, 117, 122
Public Utilities Board 92

Quaggy 90
Quays 78
Queen Elizabeth Olympic Park 103
Queens (New York) 32

Radburn 32, 33
Railways 24, 25, 29, 31, 101, 103, 105
Rainforest 71, 72
Rain gardens 72, 84–7, 89, 97, 99, 113,
   117, 118
Rainwater harvesting 84, 85, 88, 89, 124, 130
Rammed-earth 14
Recreation 36, 41, 59, 60, 79, 106
Red Data Book 131
Reductionism 55
Reductionist 5
Reed boats 8, 12
Regeneration 61, 78, 79, 91, 101
Regional planning 32, 33, 35, 36, 107, 109
Regulating services 58, 59
Regulations 5, 11, 27, 46, 85, 97, 112
Renaissance 12, 18, 133
Renault 31
Reptiles 77, 103
Reservoirs 43, 82–4, 89, 92
Resilience 52, 138
Respiratory disease 45, 83
Restoration 4, 5, 41, 57, 59, 61, 68, 78,
   79, 89–93, 102, 107, 109, 117, 132,
   133, 137, 138
Revolutionary War 23
Rice 10, 14
Richardson (Benjamin Ward) 136
Richmond Park 93
Rills 85
Rio de Janeiro 37, 52, 58
Riots 28
Ritual 11
River 4, 8–14, 17, 22, 32, 33, 42–4, 48, 50, 74,
   78, 79, 81, 83, 84, 86, 89–93, 97, 99, 103,
   105, 107, 108, 116, 123, 137, 138
River-bed 90

River corridors 78, 103
River restoration 78, 89–92
River valley 10, 11, 14, 50, 99, 103, 107
Rolls Royce factory 135
Rome 1, 3, 16, 17, 57
Royal families 11
Royal Horticultural Society 69
Royal Park (Melbourne) 88, 89
Royal Parks 41
Royal Society 20, 72
Ruhr 75
Russia 19
Rustbelt 37

Salix 99
Salmon 22, 97
Sanitarian 136
Sanitation 11, 19, 26, 28, 37, 92
Saraswati 13
Sargon 12
Saw Mill River 90
Schmidt (Marco) 129
Schools 33, 34
Schwegeler 134
Scrap 49
Sea 4, 8, 12, 43, 50, 53, 56, 82–4, 137, 138
Sea level 11, 45, 52, 56, 73, 137
Second World War 5, 34, 89, 103, 106,
   114, 132
Sediments 11, 42, 84, 89
Sedum 132
Seeding 24, 131
Segregation 33
Seine 33
Semmelweis 26
Seoul 90, 91
Seraya 71
Settlements 8, 9, 11, 13, 14, 17, 30, 37,
   116, 137
Sewage 22, 26, 43, 53, 81, 85, 99
Sewer 13, 20, 26, 28, 43, 60, 85, 97, 105, 120
Shaanxi 10
Shade 44, 72, 114, 116–18, 125, 131, 140
Shang Dynasty 13, 14
Shanghai 134
Shanxi 10
Sheet piling 78
Sheffield University 69
Shipbuilding 14

Shipping 27, 37
Shopping 27, 29, 126
Short-rotation coppice 99
Sicily 14, 16
Sienna 18
Silent Spring 56
Singapore 33, 71, 91, 92, 134
Skylark 135
Skyrise greenery 134
Skyscraper 32
Slavery 19
Slovakia 116
Slums 33, 35, 37, 116
Smog 46, 120
Smoke 26
Snow (John) 26,
Soho (London) 26
Soil 4, 5, 12, 14, 40–43, 46, 49, 53, 59, 72, 74,
    76, 82, 84–8, 93, 95, 99, 113, 118, 120, 122,
    124, 125, 127, 128, 130, 140
Songer (Kevin) 136
Soot 45, 46, 120
Sorghum 10
South America 8
South Bank 79
South Korea 91
Spain 121
Spanish colonial town planning 19
Species-rich grasslands 77
Sprawl 17, 32, 34, 35, 65, 101, 138
Squalor 21, 22
Squash 10
Squatter 116
SSSI 74, 75
Standards 26, 27, 37, 82–5, 107, 113, 123, 134
Staple Inn 19
Stapleton Airport 107, 108
Statues 13
Status 11
Steam 23, 24, 29, 50
Steel 29, 33, 48, 49, 83, 90
Stepping stone 41
Stevenage 35
Stewardship 4, 5, 49, 61
Stockton 24
Stomata 128
Stone Age 8, 11
Storm-water 44
St. Paul's Cathedral 20

St. Petersburg 19
Streets 1, 9, 15, 16, 19, 21, 26, 28, 31, 34, 42,
    86, 87, 107, 111–13, 116, 118, 119, 122
Stucki 126
Sub-saharan Africa 10
Substrate 74, 128–32, 134
Suburbs 29, 32–5
Sulphur dioxide 45, 49
Sumatra 8
Sumeria 12
Sun 63, 123, 125, 126, 128, 140
Sunnyside Gardens 32
Superior (Lake) 57
Supporting services 58, 59, 82
Surpluses 1, 11–13
Sussex 135
Sustainable development 58, 85
Sustainable Infrastructure Committee 97
Sustainable Sites Initiative 61, 62
Sustainable Urban Drainage 85, 86, 89, 120
Sutcliffe Park 90
Sutton (London Borough) 107
Suzhou 14
Swales 85, 86, 88, 118
Swallow 134
Sweden 99, 116, 123
Swift 134
Switzerland 116, 118, 125, 126, 131, 132, 135
Sylva 72

Taboo 116
Tansley (Arthur) 55
Taut (Bruno) 30
Taxation 11
Taxicabs 31
Teagle (Bunny) 69
Technical University Berlin 129
Temples 12, 13, 16, 17
Tennessee 101
Tenochtitlan 19
Teotihuacan 17
Termite 62, 63
Terrace 18
Terrain 41, 83, 95
Thames Estuary 74
Thomas Jefferson Planning District 105
Thrace 14
Tides 63
Tigris 12

Tilia 73
Timber 8, 12, 14, 19–21, 49, 135
Toba catastrophe 8
Tokyo 35
Tombs 13, 17
Tools 8
Topography 15, 17, 45, 84, 88, 118
Topsoil 41, 74
Toronto 56, 118
Totnes 77
Tower Bridge 69, 79
Town and Country Planning Association 29
Town planning 19, 26, 29, 31, 41, 86
Tracks 8, 11, 24
Tractors 51
Trade 8, 11, 14, 17, 20, 26
Traders 11
Traffic 25, 32, 41, 47, 87, 88, 91, 112, 113, 118
Trams 29
Transition 137
Transport 2, 9, 27, 37, 51, 53, 95, 103, 105
Tree Council 73
Tree pits 120, 121
Trees for Cities 120
Tree trenches 121
Trout 57
Tunnels 24, 34
Turkey 9, 134
Twelve Tables (Law of) 16
Typhoid 26

Ubaid 11
UNEP 46
United States 3, 34, 35, 52
Unwin (Raymond) 31
Uplands 11, 67, 97
Ur 12
Urban extensions 107
Urban Growth Boundaries 101
Urban Heat Islands 37, 44, 45, 93, 105, 106, 118
Urban wildlife 60, 77
Urban Wildlife Group 60
Uruk 12
USDA Forest Service 72
Uzbekistan 83

Vancouver Convention Centre 133
Vaux 26

Vegetation 4, 40, 42, 45, 46, 65, 67, 68, 74–6, 82, 84, 88, 89, 92, 93, 99, 103, 113, 122, 124, 129–32, 134, 140
Vehicles 16, 31, 37, 44–6, 48, 86, 112, 120
Versailles 19
Viaducts 24
Vickers (Denis) 69
Victoria Park 26
Vienna 26
Vines 125
Virginia 105
Virtual water 83
Vision 39, 107, 140
VOCs 46
Volcanologists 8

Walking 21, 30, 33, 79, 99, 103, 105, 113, 138
Walls 9, 12, 13, 17–19, 46, 62, 77, 78, 85, 89, 116, 122, 125–9, 134
Warehouses 27, 78
Warships 51
Waste 9, 21, 22, 49, 50, 53, 63, 124
Wasteland 68, 69, 73
Wastewater 43, 83, 92, 93, 99, 123
Water 2, 4, 5, 7, 11, 13, 16, 17, 20–24, 26, 28, 34–7, 40–44, 48, 49, 53, 56–9, 63, 67, 71, 72, 79, 81, 93, 95–7, 105, 107, 109, 116–18, 120–125, 127–30, 137, 138, 140
Water butts 85, 86
Watercourses 26, 34, 40–44, 50, 53, 70, 82, 83, 85, 89, 93, 106, 107, 137
Water cycle 42, 59, 82
Water Sensitive City 93
Water Sensitive Urban Design 72, 86
Water stress 82
Waterways 11, 36
Waterworks 28, 125
Wealth 11, 12, 17, 19
Weather 10, 11, 16, 44, 45, 52, 86, 89, 130
Weavers 11
Weeds 42
Welland (canal) 56
Wells 10, 13, 26, 48, 52, 84
Welwyn Garden City 30
Westminster 25
Wetlands 4, 26, 50, 74, 77, 81, 86, 90
Wheat 9, 10, 12, 48

Wheels 16, 17
Wilderness 40, 51
Wild grains 8
Wildlife 1, 4, 42, 43, 46, 47, 56, 60, 63,
    68–70, 72, 74, 77, 79, 86, 89–93, 99,
    101, 103, 105–7, 114, 120, 130–136,
    138, 140
Wildlife crossing 101, 105
Wildlife Trusts 69
William Curtis Ecological Park 69
Willow 99, 100
Wilson (David Sloan) 113
Wilson (E O) 4, 41
Wind 14, 41, 42, 44, 45, 63, 123,
    126, 140
Wood 14, 16, 17, 77, 78
Wood (natural historian) 66
Woodchip 135
Woonerf 112
Workforce 12
World Expo 134

Wren (Christopher) 19, 20
Writing 2, 11, 13, 14, 136

Xi'an 16

Yangshao 10
Yangtze River 14
Yellow River 14
Yemen 12
Yin Xu 14
Yokohama 35
Yonkers 90
Younger Dryas 8

Zero discharge 89, 130
Zero waste 63
Zhouzhuang 14, 15
Ziggurats 12
Zimbabwe 62–3
Zoning 29, 37
Zurich 125

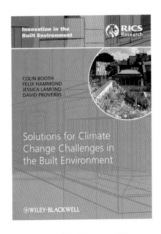

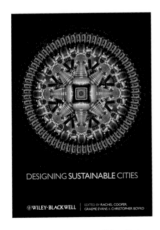
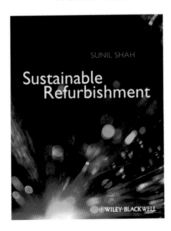
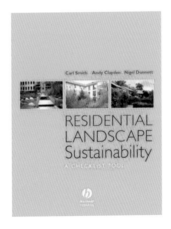